Cover Art
Hoang Hong Cam, *Country girl #4*, oil on canvas (80x100cm), 1997
Held in the private collection of Ron Burman

Sibyl James © 2005
ISBN 0-9718967-6-3

StringTown Press
P. O. Box 1406
Medical Lake WA 99022-1406
home.earthlink.net/~stringtown

Thanks to Alexandra and Star, my aging computer and printer for making it through another manuscript—and to Delilah and Jet, my new computer and printer for finishing the job. Thanks also to Artist Trust for the financial and moral support to complete this journal and to the Cultural Development Authority of King County and the Seattle Mayor's Office of Arts and Cultural Affairs for supporting the publication of this manuscript.

Ho Chi Minh's Motorbike
A Vietnam Travel Journal

Sibyl James

StringTown Press

Thy body is in jail.
But thy spirit, never.
For the great cause to prevail,
Let thy spirit soar, higher!

Ho Chi Minh, *Prison Diary*

Preface

This is a journal based on an extended trip I took to Vietnam and comprises the story of my own journey, the story of the remembered collision of the U.S. with Vietnam, and the stories of contemporary Vietnam that touch on both past and present. Geographically, the journey takes the reader from Ho Chi Minh City (Saigon) to Hanoi and back. Emotionally, it's a personal journey, encompassing my impressions of the country, my experiences as an independent traveler trying to navigate within a context of unfamiliar customs and language, my encounters with the people of present-day Vietnam and the ghosts of the past. While slightly older friends tell me their political and social consciousness was formed in the movement for civil rights, my own has its roots in the movement against the U.S./Vietnam war. "Oh, that stuff was just political," my current students tell me, as a way of dismissing their own lack of political action, thoroughly cynical about "government" and thoroughly convinced of their inability to influence its actions. "You're right," I say, "it was political. It was political when a march shut down the freeway through our city. And all the other collective actions that shut down the war." They indulge my rants. They don't believe me, really. It's difficult to believe in the power of collective action or vision when other forces keep shutting down such movements, keep enticing us to buy sport utility vehicles instead. Once upon a time, I believed in Ho Chi Minh, in his vision for Vietnam. I suppose I still do. I suppose that's why I chose to spend my vacation in Vietnam where the word "vacation" seems an anomaly—a tourist assaulting the Mekong Delta? My friend Lana, ten years younger, whose memory of the war had more to do with her father's serving in it, wanted to visit. And so, we embarked on the first obstacles of our travels: just plain getting there. I contacted a travel agent who barely spoke English. When I first called her, she told me the flights for my preferred day and every day surrounding it were full on Korean Airlines. "But," she said, "I will make a special request." I found this odd until I remembered the year I lived in China where hotels were proclaimed to be full, but if I persisted and ensconced myself in the lobby, a room miraculously appeared. I had patience with Korean Air. My tickets to Vietnam appeared just as miraculously.

August 6, Ho Chi Minh City

Few things are as disconcerting to a traveler as arriving in the target country after midnight and without hotel reservations at the time-zone stunned conclusion of a transoceanic flight. In the travel guides, these should be termed the arrivals from hell. My friend Lana and I have just disembarked in such a hell, have stepped off the plane and jammed onto the bus that has carried its international passengers across the deserted runways to the concrete walls of the airport outside Ho Chi Minh City, which everyone, most of all the locals, doggedly refers to as Saigon. We have fought for position in the shifting, shapeless mass that people in the so-called Third World name a line, and made it to the immigration desk where a short woman dwarfed by the large, black, no-nonsense frames of her glasses has sent us back to square one to have our photos taken (for a price) and fill out more papers that look suspiciously like visas (though we've already paid $60 for a visa in the States). Armed with our new documents, we elbow our way back to the immi-gration desk, only to meet another roadblock. "Hotel?" the uni-formed woman demands, pointing to a blank space in the form. "I don't know yet" is not an acceptable response. We consult the guide book, write down a name. The woman waves us through. At last, we're officially in Vietnam.

And why not let that hotel plucked randomly from the guide book be our destination? It seems as good a choice as any. Bolstered by the hyperventilated state of jet-lag, we confer in shaky English with a man who claims to drive a taxi. We agree on a price and follow him to a parking lot where he motions that we should climb into his ordinary private car. I decline, having lived for a while in Mexico and read the scandal columns in newspapers there—exposés denouncing the pirate taxis that deliver their passengers to waiting thieves. Instead, we roam the parking lot until we find a car with an actual taxi sign and re-nego-tiate the fare.

This is only the beginning. As Dante's *Inferno* makes clear, there are circles within circles in hell. In the dimness of the short ride into town, random cyclists and pedestrians and other cabs appear, flitting suddenly across the streets like cats on a full moon night. The scene reminds me of my arrival years ago in China, and I recall a story that a friend told me during the year that I taught at a college in Shanghai. Two teachers were traveling the darkened streets in a cab; one was killed and the other blinded when their taxi collided with a group of men bearing a tree trunk across the road. No matter how hard I've tried, I have never been able to imagine the configuration of this tragedy, what dangerous angle the tree-laden men could have suddenly appeared from, how a hand-carried tree could have wreaked such havoc on a passing car. Now I blot out the memory. It's safer to forget, to assume an optimistic innocence in any new country.

The driver pulls up outside an unlit run-down building that does indeed bear the name and address of the hotel listed in our guide book. He begins unloading luggage while Lana and I mill about in front of the building's chain-fenced door. "Mill about" may seem an exaggeration for only two people, but given all the different time-zone versions of ourselves that we're still inhabiting, we think we deserve a crowd-sized verb. The two men sitting in the bat-infested dark surrounding the hotel's door wave their arms in negative arcs. The hotel is not only closed for the night. It is full. The same is true of the next hotel that the men direct the driver to. And by this time, any man still lounging on the city's streets has insinuated himself into our search for lodging, crowding scrappily beside the taxi's doors while every late-night beggar is busy trying to insert his palm inside the small crack that we've established for air in the backseat window. The taxi driver calls into headquarters for a possible address and gets only static. From my purse, I dig out a shred of paper with the names of hotels where somebody else that I vaguely know has stayed, hotels outside the limits of our bare-bones budget, which is based on finding rooms in the $10-20 range that our guide book swears is possible. We promise the driver an extra Yankee dollar if he'll just keep searching, and name a street.

When the cab pulls over beside a darkened row of buildings, there's no neon hotel sign, not even an entrance, only a blank metal wall the size of a garage door. The driver locates a buzzer and jams his thumb against it until the steel wall rolls up to reveal a middle-aged woman in pajamas asking a late-night, take-it-or-suffer price. The place is called the Business Hotel; the woman is clearly taking her cue from the name. I convince Lana that the passage out of hell is priceless. We sign the register, hand over our several visas. And now that we've agreed to become her guests, the proprietor softens, assuring us that this deal is only for tonight, that tomorrow she'll manage to move us to some more affordable quarters.

Upstairs, in our spacious but dankly concrete room, the maid has left a neatly folded towel at the foot of each bed. The towels are thick and over-sized, the sort you'd carry to the beach. Mine features a portrait of Tinker Bell; Lana's has a scene from *Beauty and the Beast*. Disney has preceded us to Vietnam.

On the bathroom sink lies the first of the large pink plastic combs that I will find are standard hotel-issue fare, an amenity like those tiny bottles of shampoo and conditioner in hotels in the States. Only I suspect these combs are not replaced as often as the bottles of shampoo; I suspect they remain the same, a fixture permanent as the beds or chairs, used by visitor after visitor, like the hard plastic slippers stationed beside the wooden wardrobe that serves as a closet. I have no interest in using this comb. Later, when I've noted the frequency of street scenes of women sitting with the head of a friend or a child in their laps, checking for lice, my lack of interest in such combs will take on more serious proportions. But for now, I'm simply not interested. I want to take a shower, not comb my hair. I pick up the white cardboard wrapper whose pristine condition guarantees that the soap is changed after each guest leaves. Below a festive blue and yellow design, the wrapper sports its brand name: General Tourist Soap. The Business Hotel, General Tourist Soap. Maybe everything about the country is generic. Or maybe it's only Lana and I who have fallen into that category. We like to think of ourselves as unique, but for the next month, we'll be strictly tourists, washing the grime from our generically foreign bodies, our individual souls reduced to travel bureau statistics, priming the economy with our tiny cache of faceless dollars.

August 6, (STILL!!) Ho Chi Minh City

This is what it means to cross the international date line. The day you've lost continues endlessly into the next. We haven't really slept after our midnight arrival. We've simply lain in our beds, listening to the whine of the air conditioner and tiny ice box, until it seemed logical to get up. It's just past seven in the morning, and in the park across the street, the Vietnamese are already busy at their exercises, which seem to consist of soccer and badminton played without a net, nothing so exotic as those Sunday travel-spread photos of crowds of Chinese elders bending gracefully in the moves of Tai Chi.

We load up on sun screen and hats, stumble down the concrete stairs to find the manager of our hotel who's still in her striped cotton pajamas. She pats the permanent wave in her black curls, adjusts her glasses, and consults the register. A cheaper room won't be available till tomorrow, but for now she'll discount the one we're in. Apparently, the country hasn't yet sold its soul to rampant capitalism, despite the invasion of Western businessmen anxious to found joint ventures, to exploit this new pool of cheap but talented and resourceful laborers. Business matters concluded, the manager is now ready to provide us with instructions, her manner alternating between bossiness and genuine concern. Within minutes, we begin to think of her as our Vietnamese mother, a little pushy in her insistence on commanding oversight of her children's welfare (a pushiness we'll eventually come to appreciate). She tells us where to find a bank to change our dollars. She loans us some Vietnamese dong so that we can pay a driver to ferry us to the bank in his cyclo—a hybrid contraption reminiscent of rickshaws, featuring two-thirds of a bicycle fronted by a wide seat for passengers and cargo, set between two tall wheels. The seat sports a metal foot-rest and struts rising into a collapsible canopy. The cyclo is simultaneously a feat of efficient engineering and a reminder that this is a labor-intensive world dependent on the strong hearts and calves of its population.

Our Vietnamese mama cautions us concerning just how much the ride should cost; then she sketches out the route, and makes us a gift of her only map. "The bank is not so far from here. Both of you can take one cyclo." And we do, Lana sitting a little forward in the seat so I can squeeze in beside her. We're thankful that neither of us is very large. We suspect the cyclo driver is even more thankful.

Surprisingly, banks in Vietnam are at least as modernly computerized as their counterparts in the States. And have at least as many rules. We discover that we can't change our travelers checks because we haven't brought along the receipts, those papers that the issuing banks always caution you to carry separately from the checks themselves. But in a less-than-official office down the street, this lack of documents is no problem. The exchange rate leaves us armed with brick-sized stacks of Vietnamese dong. And so hungry that we don't care that the nearest cafe is a tourist haven. At its rear, a kind of open courtyard houses the door to the funky toilet, flushed by filling a red bucket with water from the sink. Beside the toilet lies the kitchen, with women tending plucked chickens above a charcoal fire, chopping vegetables, washing dishes in plastic tubs on the cement floor. Out front, the cafe is packed with visitors negotiating tours, digging into Western-style omelets, slathering their baguettes with nostalgic peanut butter and jam, while consulting their copies of the Lonely Planet's survival guide to Vietnam, which is currently the only comprehensive travel guide in English, and one that we'll soon find the Vietnamese have memorized—at least the sections pertaining to their own place of business.

Lana and I, of course, already have our own copy of this guide, and guiltily fend off the gaunt children intent on selling us another one—or at least a stack of postcards or a phrase book. (After I've returned home, I'll run into employees from the Lonely Planet press at a book fair. Those guides sold in Vietnam, they'll tell me, are clever facsimiles, plagiarized versions with some sections left out. Vietnam, like so many Asian nations, ignores the rules of international copyrights. The Lonely Planet staff have more or less given up the battle over ownership, have settled for petitioning for a share of the local sales. Whether they'll get even a cut of the take is doubtful. But, at this moment, I think the guide in the hand of a six-year-old vendor is legitimate—just the first of the goods I'll refuse to buy in Vietnam.)

The cyclo drivers are more difficult to resist. One of them chats us up, offering a tour of the city, feeling us out to determine just what sort of sights we're interested in. He seems kindly gentle, honest and reliable, his face already flushed by the day's heat under a thatch of black hair. Beneath his Bermuda shorts, his stocky calves testify to his years of experience in peddling heavy loads. A host of other cyclo drivers, less fluent in English, hang silently about while we settle on an itinerary and an hourly price, then our multilingual man hails one of them—a skinny youngster dragging on his cigarette—and we're off.

I have to admit that this cyclo business makes me uneasy. Being driven about in a sort of carriage or cart attached to the front of a bike seems too much like riding in a rickshaw, the privilege of some mon-eyed foreigner or local aristocrat in China, in the days before Mao and the Long March. But in Vietnam, it seems that anyone who doesn't own a motorbike uses a cyclo. Even cows are riding past in them on their way to market. I try to stop worrying about the strain on the cyclists' knees. Instead, I worry about my own safety. In a cyclo, the passengers seated up front feel as if the entire thrust of Vietnamese unruly traffic is coming toward them. And it is.

We've agreed on a three-hour tour, with a list of designated sites. But suddenly glimpsing a building roofed with multicolored figures, I point, and we're already off into more than our planned itinerary. But so what? It turns out to be one of the only Hindu temples in the city, and who would have expected to find a Hindu temple in Vietnam? Our cyclo guide knows everything, knows which temples demand that we shed our shoes to enter and which don't, knows which allow tourist photos. He understands the rhythm of our steps, when we'll stop to investigate and admire, when we'll forage on, already surfeit with curiosities. Leaving the Hindu worshippers lighting incense before the painted many-armed gods and goddesses inhabiting their altars, we make another detour, this time to the crumbling cement of the monolithic edifice that our guide calls "the building of the thousand eyes." It's the old American embassy, studded all over with windows set be-tween x-shaped patterns of concrete, a place given its thousand-eye name, our guide says, by the Vietnamese who thought the U.S. could see everything they did. In some tasteless bureaucratic version of the red canopies that shelter the approach to posh hotels, the sidewalk leading to the door is covered by a long stretch of delapidated concrete "awning" through which a tree has forced its way. Neither this building nor the nearby equally vacant British embassy has been trashed. They simply vegetate, in the state in which their occupants abandoned them, monuments to power or its defeat, waiting for the next move in the game.

We get back to our real itinerary, which consists mostly of Buddhist temples because Lana is a devotee and I don't really care what we visit, just happy to be truly in Vietnam and grateful to be semi-functional after so many hours without real sleep. Inside the Emperor of Jade Pagoda, we're greeted by huge porcelain figures of the emperor and his cohorts, figures engagingly doll-like and full of expression around their long beards. On the balcony, a laughing buddha, with his rotund belly ballooning nakedly through his robes, throws up his arms like a Master of Ceremonies announcing the beginning of the show. The room behind him features minature three-dimensional likenesses of a host of robbers who learned the error of their ways and went straight. We descend the stairs to a small statue wearing what seems to be a chef's hat, a man to whom you pray for money. "Everybody," says our guide, "comes to the temples to ask for money." Or for fertility—a prayer to be answered in the alcove headed by a female buddha surrounded by rows of tiny ceramic women holding children, feeding babies at their breasts. Every statue is fraught with detail; everything has a childlike air of playfulness.

We go on to Giac Lam, an old temple set amidst the tombs of monks—the longer you've been a monk, the bigger and grander your tomb. From the balconies of nearby tenements, children hail us as we wander the cemetary's stone monuments bearing designs incorporating the swastika which was peacefully Buddhist till Hitler turned it into a symbol of evil. Inside the temple, there's a darkness unrelieved by the weight of mahogany furniture. We sip tea from a tray holding a pot and cups used over and over by the day's visitors, nothing but the holiness of the atmosphere to wash the germs from the cup's rim. We admire the "buddha tree" shaped like a coat rack, hung with figures of the buddha like Christmas ornaments. An elderly monk in his robe and shaved head joins us, asks us the usual questions concerning our origins and names and age—and refuses to believe me when I swear that I'm nearly fifty. I wonder if this is the equivalent of monkish flirtation. He tosses back his glass of tea like a shot of tequila and we all shake hands.

Along one exterior wall, there are scenes of hell or purgatory detailing crimes and their designated punishment: the woman who took two husbands at once is sawed in half; the man who killed a bear is turned into one. In the lecture hall, serious-minded monks and nuns and students listen and take notes. Behind that, there's the kitchen filled with big copper pots where a scrawny grey kitten paces between the rows of long wooden tables, waiting for them to be filled, for a friendly leg to rub, a careless diner to drop a bit of rice or fish. Annexed to the kitchen is a room stocked with shelves of painted ceramic jars that I imagine must be a giant aesthetically pleasing pantry. But I find that it's a giant funerary instead, its shelves storing not rice but cremated remains in lotus-shaped vases adorned with photos of the deceased. My error reminds me to take no assumption as certain.

What's certain is the afternoon downpour greeting us outside the temple. The drivers unfurl the hoods on their cyclos, cover us with big heavy cloths like those lead aprons that dental assistants place across their clients before they take an x-ray.

At the Quan Am Pagoda, the rain has stopped, and the country's penchant for ceramic design has hit its height. Monkeys, turtles, dragons, fish, lions, humans and buddhas populate its roof. Lana combs a heap of broken roof decor, filling her bag with bits of tails and claws, the nose of a buddha, a goddess's rosy cheek—pieces to include in her next sculpture. (A month later, waiting in the airport's customs line, we'll read the list of things we're not allowed to export, including "antiques and sacred images." No problem, we'll say, considering our tiny cache of cheap souvenirs and local old lady second-hand clothes. Then we'll remember the bag of temple trash. But Lana is a charmed woman. On the way in to the country, she was reading a book banned in Vietnam; on the way out, she'll be smuggling sacred bits of garbage. The handcuffs won't close around our wrists; the officials won't even ask us to unzip our bags.)

The Quan Am is what I call the "beauty salon" temple, peopled with female attendants ready to enhance your existence, to perform whatever ritual is dictated by your needs, whether that be a yen for marriage or fertility or just to get rid of bad luck. Beggars line the entrance, beside vendors with cages of small birds that worshippers can buy and release as a prayer. Across the street, stalls supply the necessary paraphernalia: incense, packets of colored papers, stick figures wearing paper clothes (or you can bring your own real garments to burn to banish bad luck). Roosters and hens roam the temple; ponds hold turtles symbolizing good luck; the smoke from incense creates small clusters of fog. At a repectful distance, I watch one attendant position a cone made of bamboo struts above a petitioner's head, then medthodically brush a handful of ritual papers against the cone. I know I'm in a temple but the scene reminds me of the way my hairdresser and I stare into the mirror as the latest cut is blown dry into an image I'll have to wear, a moment that has all the intensity of prayer.

Lana and I wander from altar to altar, not sure what future we should pray for, sure that we'll return on the stopover before we head for home to purchase boxes of the hanging coils of incense that spiral from the ceiling like thin brown chandeliers.

Our guide thinks we've been purified enough. "You like rivers?" he asks and steers us toward the shores where boats arrive from the Mekong Delta, most of them laden with bananas. Some of those ripening bunches will end up on temple altars, the yellow crescents curved skyward like a mammoth blossom with a rosy dragon fruit or green-skinned orange placed at the center. Lana and I amass a crowd when we alight from the cyclos beside the river, the denizens of the boats intrigued even though we're simply generic tourists. And we're intrigued by the enormous eyes painted on the bows of their wooden crafts, though I can't quite decide whether the guide is explaining that the eyes are meant to resemble big fish (and thus attract a good catch) or to scare them off (thus ridding the waves of sea monsters).

It's been eight hours since we left that tourist cafe. I'm exhausted. I don't even want to imagine how the men peddling our cyclos feel. In the last pink blush of sunset, we pull up to the Business Hotel with only business left to be transacted. There's really no way to reward these men for what they've given us today. I know that the silent cyclo driver smokes. I suspect that mine does too, or at least could turn some American cigarettes into a good bargain. I hand him my nearly full pack and the payment for the day's excursion in dollars not dong. Lana and I try out the Vietnamese he's been trying to teach us as we tell our respective drivers thank you and good-bye. It's early enough that the door to the hotel is still a door, not a metal wall. We wave and walk inside. "Have a good time?" our Vietnamese mama asks. "Not so far from here," she adds, "is a place where you can eat a good dinner."

August 7, Ho Chi Minh City

I'm standing on a corner in Saigon, now known as Ho Chi Minh City, and can't bring myself to step off the curb. Crossing the street seems like a suicidal act. To be sure, there are not that many cars and, if I concentrate, I can dodge the cyclos. But there is a solid onslaught of motorbikes, revving their engines, darting constantly and threateningly past. These are not the funky mo-peds that I usually associate with so-called underdevelopment where vehicles advance at a manageable putt-putt pace. These bikes are the real thing, with real horsepower.

Now and then, a whole family passes, with dad manning the gears, mom and the kids stacked behind him. But mostly, the motorbikes are piloted by young men in American baseball caps or young women in everything from Western dress to the country's traditional fashion of delicate silk or nylon pants and matching long side-buttoned tunics known as ao dais. Whatever their style of dress, these young women have one intent in common: they want to retain their skin's pale blossom; they don't want to acquire a tan. To ensure this end, they've encased their arms in long over-the-elbow cotton gloves, the sort that an American girl would have worn to a high school prom in the fifties; on their heads, they wear broad-brimmed felt hats or straw boaters sashed with bright ribbons as gaily innocent as Rebecca of Sunny Brook Farm. I call them the belles of Vietnam. Their wardrobes strike me as engagingly demure. Their driving styles terrorize me.

It's not surprising that most of the motorbike drivers are young. I've read that the large majority of the country's population is under 25. So far, my own observations have confirmed that there are not that many old men or women on the streets and not many in the middle-aged category to which I would reluctantly assign myself. In the U.S.-Vietnam war, hundreds of thousands of soldiers died, and around four million civilians (ten percent of Vietnam's population) were killed or wounded. I don't like to think about the war, the casualties that might account for the current shortage of the elderly and semi-elderly. I try to focus on the present where the streets are powered by an energy mostly birthed after the years of the U.S.-Vietnam conflict. It's possible that this generation is not encumbered by a history that—in order to get on with the business of living—they've been obliged to forgive and forget. It's also possible that, unlike me, they're not carrying the baggage of earlier revolutionary visions that they regret the present hasn't fulfilled. I'm dismayed by the country's rapid Westernization that's so raucously symbolized by motorbikes. But the owners of those noisy symbols appear delighted.

The horde of motorbikes masses at the streetlight, some of them roaring through the intersection no matter whether the light is red or green, all of them seemingly fueled by the infiltration of baseball caps and Coca Cola. I imagine the ghost of Ho Chi Minh turning over in his mausoleum, aghast at the outcome of his years of struggle. I hesitate on the curb, sure that I'm not ready to die for this motorized present, uncertain about whether I'd have sacrificed my life to fend it off.

1968, The Democratic Convention

These days, déjà vu occurs whenever I'm partaking in a political demonstration and the crowd begins to chant, "The whole world's watching." That chant always transports me back to 1968, Chicago, and the
Democrats' presidential convention—the first time I heard those ad-
monishing words. I don't know whether the whole world was watching the police attacking the demonstrators outside the convention,
but for once the media's cameras were trained on the action, and
certainly I was watching. I wasn't physically present at those dem-
onstrations; I was at my parents' home in central Illinois—a world
away from Chicago which always seemed like a separate state to
me. I sat on the floor in front of the television, fashioning what I
called a "hate collage," a collection of magazine and newspaper
photos detailing such things as the atrocities of the war on Vietnam
and the U.S. perpetrators.

I was barely twenty-two. Like many others at my university, I'd
taken to wearing an old green army jacket, donned not in support of the
war but as a symbol of dissent. In the student cafeteria, I had sat at the
table frequented by members of the Students for a Democratic Society
(SDS) but I was really only a fellow traveler then. And a critic, attend-
ing SDS meetings with a friend and later laughing about the solemn
testimonials of the members. Born on Bastille Day, I came to believe in
myself as destined to be a radical, but I think it was the Democratic
Convention that sent me over the edge into real political action. And
maybe that's the wonderful thing about Democrats—for all their fail-
ings. At least the wonderful thing about Democrats in 1968. It was
THEIR convention that people thought worth protesting at, THEIR
venue where dissent might get a hearing, even if the whole world wasn't
watching. Inside the convention center, the band was playing "Hello
Dolly" and "Happy Days Are Here Again." Outside, there were em-
battled demonstrators intent on proving these were not happy days.

I know now I was a privileged radical. I was white, a college
student, and female. I wasn't going to be drafted. I had more in

common with Abbey Hoffman and the Yippies' brand of street theatre protest than with the Black Panthers who were paying attention to the idea that all politics is local—and being gunned down by the government for their efforts.

August 7, Heading Out of Ho Chi Minh City

On the bus driver's cassette player, Rod Stewart is rhythmically pro-claiming that this is a beautiful Sunday, a beautiful day. And it will be, though the morning's thicket of clouds hasn't burned off yet, and the bus is honking through a denser thicket of mopeds, motorbikes, and cyclos. On the edges of the city, there's a frenzy of home-building. The construction rises in increments. First, the basic foundation—a con-crete square about the size of two average rooms. Later, when there's sufficient money, a second floor will be added, maybe even a third. Meanwhile, the structural bits of steel protrude like antennae from what-ever ceiling currently functions as the roof. Smaller, less optimistic houses end in sheets of corrugated tin, rows of clay tiles, or whatever the enterprising homeowner has found to nail against the weather.

The bus seems to hurtle past, though any speed seems break-neck in a vehicle in what's called the underdeveloped world. The driver honks his horn incessantly, laying on it in a sassy "I'm coming, watch out" percussion. I'd like to commandeer the streets the way he does, all my flags flying, passing everything in sight to the beat of "It's a Beautiful Day."

We pass a cemetery of military graves in their plots as organized as suburban subdivisions. It's the same everywhere: the more disorderly your death, the more orderly the society tries to make your final resting place. I prefer the honest chaos of the countryside we're entering now, where clusters of graves sprout like mushrooms in clumps or disparate scatters. Humble crumbly brown markers in the shape of lotus buds surround grander tombs that take the curving sweep of Oriental divans, some with awnings of faux marble—or maybe it's real marble or just snazzy concrete. At this distance, I can't be sure. In one village, I see coffins being made in a shop: plain wooden lozenges, sometimes lay-ered with a veneer of bright decorations like the shiny blue and red and silver foil of Christmas.

Beside the coffin shop, rows of rectangles surrounding woven circles have been propped against the trees—maybe a tool for sifting rice, maybe the rice pancakes themselves, set out in the sun to dry before they're carried to the table, dunked in a dish of water to soften till they can be rolled around some pork and shrimp and vegetables and dipped into the spicy, salty fish sauce, the omnipresent nuoc mam. I'd like to ask our day's tour guide about the meaning of these scenes outside the bus's window, but he's a sleazy, skinny, useless man with nearly indecipherable English who tells us nothing about anything we see unless it relates to war, the only subject that makes his eyes gleam. "I used to work," he says, "for the Americans." Now, he's announcing the significance of the bridge we're crossing. "It was here," he says, "that someone tried to assassinate Robert MacNamara." He consults his notes. Apparently they remind him that it's time again to praise the Americans. And so he does.

Why praise the Americans, I wonder. The folks who brought you napalm and Agent Orange. Who brought you bomb craters swampy now with the malaria of mosquitoes. The troops who brought you hard currency in exchange for the bodies of your women. The country that brought you Coca-Cola and is now hell-bent on bringing you capitalism. Why praise the Americans? And why damn your own people, as every guide I've encountered has done so far, damning the commies, the North Vietnamese, the government of reunification. This particular guide spews so much propaganda that it seems as if the war has never ended. But if the current government's grip is as awful and iron-handed as he makes it out to be, why isn't he in jail for sedition, for not toeing the party line? Unfortunately it seems as if this IS the new party line. As if the government's encouraging the damning of itself, the praising of the Americans. Is this simply a strategy to lure joint ventures? Has the government agreed to say anything in return for foreign currency? Later, when we're visiting the tunnels around Cu Chi, the elaborate network of underground passages and rooms where the locals hid during the war, I talk with another guide who informs me that my guide hails from Cu Chi. His relatives huddled in the tunnels while he worked for the Americans who were desperate to destroy the population in Cu Chi by any means necessary, bombing them into oblivion or poisoning the tunnels' air holes. So which side was my guide on? Has he ever had a side? His sheerly orgasmic excitement at everything military from barbed wire gates to the poisoned spikes of booby traps makes it seem that he's on the side of mayhem, no matter who's doing it to whom or why. The lyrics of that song by Country Joe and the Fish come to mind: "And it's one, two, three, what are we fightin' for? Don't ask me, I don't give a damn." He's that kind of man.

Lana and I hadn't wanted to come to Cu Chi. Before we left the States, we'd agreed that we'd skip the tourist war sights. Both of us felt we'd had enough of the war that we'd protested at the time, and enough of its lingering aftermath, an aftermath that drove the U.S. into carpet-bombing Iraq, just to prove that it couldn't be defeated by another Third World country—another war that we'd protested. This time, we wanted to experience the country itself, in a context of peace. But a visit to the Cao Dai temple was high on our list, and all the bus tours insisted on including a trip to Cu Chi. Religion and war. It was a package deal.

At first we think we'll just wait out the stop on the bus, but then curiosity gets the better of us, and we follow the tour into the museum where we catch the tail-end of another lecture by our guide, glorifying South Vietnam, the Americans, and the instruments of war. Holding up a poisoned stake, he smiles; his eyes sparkle. It's a relief when he's followed by an old 1967 North Vietnamese propaganda film which centers mostly on the heroism of the women of Cu Chi, who worked the fields whenever the bombs weren't falling, who set traps and dynamited tanks, and received awards for killing Americans. I can't condone the idea of bounty hunting, but I'm impressed by the determination of these women and by the spirit of the villagers in general, reflected in the photos lining the walls. They lived underground, in passages too small to stand up in. And still, they built not only a subterrenean hospital, but also a school. Literacy is always part of any grassroots revolution. If you know how to read, you know what you're up against. If you can read between the lines, you can take a stand.

Outside the museum, bending over one of the entrances to the tunnels—a hole the size of a large shoe box—I can't understand how the villagers managed to overcome the claustrophobia of descent, let alone the days and nights inside the earth. The guide motions us to an entrance that's been enlarged for the big-boned bodies of Westerners. It still appears dauntingly snug. Lana and I are probably the only ones on the tour who could fit fairly easily into the hole, but we decline, watch our hunkier compatriots wedge themselves in. Some of these tunnels led into the nearby former American base; Vietnamese soldiers crawling through them appeared suddenly from nowhere to fire and then disappeared, a nightmare phantom of terror.

Walking through the area of the tunnels, I feel my skin crawl, the creepiness of flesh in a horror movie. I don't trust the guide's assurances that there is no longer any unexploded ordinance in the brush; besides, the Vietnamese tour organizers have booby-trapped the place with their own strings, so the tourists constantly set off rounds from planted cap guns. It's not my idea of a joke. How could it be theirs?

At the end, we gather in an underground "cafeteria" to taste some manioc, a kind of sweet potato that the villagers were sometimes reduced to subsisting on. The white root resembles a candle with a stringy wick running through it; it tastes exactly like wax. I have to carry my portion out into the sunlight to examine it, to be sure I haven't picked up a candle by mistake. It's a root, all right, maybe a metaphor for the sort of food a revolution is reduced to—eating its own torch to keep going.

When I picture the maps of the tunnels, the ingenuity of the Vietnamese astounds me. What astounds me more is their endurance: their small bodies compounded of wiry muscle; their equally wiry wills. And their apparent lust for life. Today, they're busy forgetting the war, focusing on the present, despite the maimed, the curse of dioxins, the forests so destroyed and dusty around places like Cu Chi.

August 7, the Cao Dai Temple

When the bus finally arrives at the Cao Dai compound, I realize that the Disney images on our hotel towels were maybe a warning. There's something Disney-like about the Cao Dai temple too, partly because of its larger-than-life scale in this land of diminutive people, and partly because of the insistent pink and blue of its obsessive decor, with columns made of spiraling dragons and a huge globe at the altar's end, dominated by the pyramid of an all-seeing third eye. But this is serious Disney, an intently religious fantasy, a carnival of faith lodged in an earthly world, celebrating both the delights of nature and the imaginative possibilities of heaven. Quick-winged swifts flit from niche to niche, and worshippers line up outside to enter, shedding their shoes, each sex entering from a different door, then sitting cross-legged in rows indicating which of the nine steps to heaven that they've attained. "Marshalls" check to be sure the faithful have settled themselves correctly, with the proper space between them, their backs straight.

Cao Dai is an eclectic religion, fusing the secular with the religious philosophies of East and West. A little of everything comes together here: Buddhism, Confucianism, Hinduism, Taoism, local spiritualism, Christianity, and Islam. The religion's contacted spirits include Joan of Arc, Descartes, Shakespeare, Victor Hugo, Louis Pasteur, and Lenin. If I had to ascribe to a sect, I'd be tempted to try this one. While the worshippers assemble, the tourists roam the aisles, snapping photos, but as the service begins, we're relegated to the less-intrusive space of the balconies reserved for visitors. I keep my eye on the only female "arch-bishop," an aged woman in a high turban with a flowing veil that falls over her shoulders, but not her face. She's sitting motionless near the front, in what surely must be the closest step to heaven. Since the moment of entering the sanctuary, she has carried a small space of dignity, a quiet power that surrounds her.

The worshipers make a dizzying sea of white silk pants and tunics, with elaborate headgear reminiscent of the courtliest Shakespearean garb mixed with Scheherazade's *Arabian Nights*. They do not appear to consider themselves or the large temple bedecked with images and color to be exotic. They do not appear to consider themselves. They pray, seemingly oblivious to the constant flux of tourists, the click of cameras.

August 8, Eye Troubles

Last night, by the time we got back to the city, my eyes were in rebellion, having become a repository for the road dust whipped through the bus windows. Trapped beneath my contact lenses, the particles of grit had set up a painful friction; my eyes produced streams of tears, trying to cleanse themselves. They kept on weeping while I washed my lenses at a restaurant, waiting for my noodles to arrive, aware of my none-too-clean fingers but knowing I needed my artificially assisted sight to lead me through the dim unfamiliar streets back to our hotel. I deluged my eyes with some product supposed to soothe them. Nothing worked. My corneas felt like flames.

I left home with a minor redness in my right eye, possibly caused by some bacteria contracted while swimming in Lake Washington. "Nothing serious," my doctor had assured me and given me some prescription drops to use in the unlikely event that my condition should get worse. "I think it will clear up in a day or two." Back in our room, I instantly removed my offending lenses, slathered my eyes with the drops my doctor had provided. This morning, my left eye is normal; the whites of my right one are purple. A small mass of crusty particles has seeped from the corner and solidified like a yellow glacier on my cheek. I steel myself and insert my lenses, accepting the pain like a woman who knows her fashionable stiletto heels are too high and the toes pinch, but she's willing to suffer to look beautiful at this party. If I blink almost constantly, I find I can generate enough tears to make the discomfort bearable. It will clear up in a day or two, I tell my reflection in the mirror, trying to sound as confidently reassuring as my doctor.

August 8, On Our Way to Dalat

I know these people are poor but the countryside appears prosperous and lushly green; the homes rarely seem run-down. The materials they're fashioned from seem to change with the geography as we travel, but the sense of care remains constant, the impulse to create design even in the simplest mud house or the square domains constructed of long planks of wood, with pitched roofs overhanging a porch like the storefronts in some Wild West movie town. The newer concrete homes are covered with textured stucco or blocks of colored stone. Everywhere, there's that urge to design, so each dwelling resembles some decorative bit of art adorned with clean lines, accented by carved stars, butterfly or daisy patterns, not too much of anything, just tasteful highlights.

I'm feeling the frustration of being always in a moving vehicle when I'm in the countryside, of not being able to take an unblurred photo, having to trust my increasingly Swiss-cheesed memory to carry these images of the country back to the States. My friends will get a skewed vision from my snapshots—all of them taken in cities. They'll miss the fresh green beauty of these rice fields and the women in conical hats wading through them, the water buffaloes, the brown humps of the Brahma cattle.

It's a country of rivers. Crossing one, we pass some humbly thatched houseboats. Crossing another, we see banks packed with actual boats, their curved wooden hulls brushed with primary colors, and round baskets attached to them that function as dinghys. One boy is crossing the river in such a basket, paddling with his hands.

It's a country of dust. There's grit in the baguettes vended beside the road (even in the loaves wrapped sometimes in plastic); grit in the bowl of rice being served on the cafe table surrounded by low stools; grit in my eyes and mouth, in the lacquer of the coffin being stained now beside the road while the bus kicks up its own dust devils.

North of Ho Chi Minh City, there's a run of massive new Christian churches, as frequent as the espresso carts that line every corner of my own latte-obsessed city of Seattle, each church big enough to house far more than the population of the village it borders. A testimony to missionary finances and zeal. I find their burgeoning presence opressive—the religious equivalent of Coca-Cola and motorbikes. Like the Western entrepreneurs, the missionaries are vying for the souls of the population, intent on reshaping them into a Western mold. I'm glad I made it to Vietnam while it was still Vietnam. I'm glad I won't live to see the world acquire the sameness of a MacDonald's franchise.

Despite the dust and heat, the women vendors manage to look fresh. And the clothes spread for sale beside the road miraculously appear clean, the pants perfectly creased. Only the men lack that look of cleanliness, that well-kept air. Lounging in their baggy shirts and equally baggy pants, and dragging on their cigarettes, they've made a quick study of how to be Westernly obnoxious, hawking after foreign women. Mercifully, some of them retain their shyness, their innocently sweet smiles.

About halfway to Dalat, the bus climbs into a jungle luxuriant with greenery, rivers, waterfalls, and valleys patched with red earth. We pass constant road shrines filled with candles and incense. In the field stands either a bodhisattva or the holy virgin; from this distance, it's hard to tell one graceful sweep of a sacred body from another.

Around Dalat, a scrub pine forest rises above the red-soiled valleys, encircling resort homes reminiscent of Swiss chalets that line the lake where tourists rent paddle boats shaped like swans—along the dock, the swan necks of the boats line up, each with a slightly individual bent to its painted neck. It's a fantasy set-up, a background where honeymooners pose, where the military brass from both north and south vacationed during the war, and there was an implicit pact not to bomb the area. We'd expected a small unspoiled village set amidst a natural wonderland. We get an expanding town with a busy market, construction cranes rising against the horizon, dust rising from the guys on motorbikes who gather around the tourist bus stop like vultures.

We eschew the Disney-like Valley of Love where visitors don cowboy costumes for photos. Instead, we haul our picnic lunch up the road away from the motorbikes, following the back paths through pines beside what are now military guest houses, and claim the grassy grounds behind some homes with a view of the valley. Halfway through our feast of rice pancakes and fruit, two men arrive on bikes. Oh no, we think, ready for some sexist confrontation. But they're not here to flirt or badger us into a tour of the city. They live here, in these small homes hugging the cliffs. And they're too shy to shoo us off. We peel another apple, watching them confer in low tones, contemplating what to do about this new breed of foreigners that have peacefully invaded, picnicking outside their door.

August 9, Dalat

Dalat is the only place where we've been cold in Vietnam. When we arrived, we found threadbare quilts on the wooden frames of our beds; we asked for sheets, and got two flowered table cloths. We shivered through the night, the heavy blue mosquito netting over our beds no use against the high-altitude chill.

This morning, we're scouting the markets, in search of warmer clothes. I buy a jeans jacket in a shop, and just outside, a Vietnamese guy offers to purchase it, thinking it's a genuine U.S. article. Made in Vietnam, I say, gesturing toward the shop, you can pick up one just like it for a song. Less official clothing markets spill down the steps outside a covered hall where "everyday things" like plastic buckets and bolts of cheap cloth serve the locals' needs. Lana begins to rummage through the stacks of secondhand clothes, and suddenly the cops arrive. Everybody scatters. Apparently, the sidewalk vendors need a license; apparently, nobody has one. For a few minutes, the police chase one woman vendor; then they disappear, and the street market scene reassembles. We wander away to investigate the flights of market steps that feature produce; we buy some rice cakes blackened over a fire, a bag of raw peanuts, a kilo of petaled dragon fruit.

Toting our purchases up the stairs to our hotel room, we're accosted by a slim man in shiny pants and a mismatched sports coat. "You do speak English," he says. It's not exactly a question. "Would you please agree to converse with our English class?" Lana gives me a nudge, indicating that she'll sit in back for moral support. I'm a teacher of English as a second or foreign language; I do this kind of thing for a living. I take a look at the man's text which features a dialogue by some girls from London who've never encountered a world outside the chimes of Big Ben. I immediately sabotage his lesson plan. His students are all employees of our cheap hotel; I've already run into some of them hanging up sheets and towels on the roof ledge where I spread my own inglorious laundry of t-shirts, cotton underpants, and Bermuda shorts that will never be really white again. Instead of asking the students to recite what those English girls do at the beach, I lean on the big bust of Lenin that graces the room and ask them their names, what they've been up to lately, and what do they really think of the tourists they serve. I'll speak in Vietnamese, I say, and you should answer in English. When we try this, my skills are so pathetic that the students turn instantly confident, so assured of their own foreign language talent that they can laughingly encourage my attempts to wrap my tongue around their country's tones. Meanwhile, Lana engages the Vietnamese teacher in English conversation, trying to distract him from worrying about the havoc I'm wreaking on his lesson plans. The ploy is only half successful. It turns out that the teacher's grip on English is too tenuous to support a lengthy discussion.

Dalat is not only the first place where we've been cold; it's also the first spot where we've seen wines and fancier, harder sorts of spirits for sale. We're not so sure of their authenticity. The shop offers a normally expensive imported liquer for a rockbottom price, but the bottle seems particularly dusty, and not quite full, as if it has already been sampled. Lana and I settle on a fifth of local red that costs the equivalent of two U.S. dollars; the tourists that we've just met in a restaurant over a dinner of sugar cane shrimp decide to purchase a similar bottle. The male member of this tourist pair seems perhaps too self-important, but Ziggy, his German companion, is an actress and endlessly entertaining in a style that's at once downhome and boisterously flamboyant. So, we invite them back to our room. The four of us stumble down the outside hallway that leads to our door, feeling our way through the night's sudden lack of electic power, aiming our flashlights toward the key hole that, for several minutes, stubbornly resists our key. The wine turns out to be an evil red, as cloyingly sweet as a jug of Mogen David or Thunderbird, the sort of bottle that should have been swigged from beneath the cover of a brown paper bag. The next day, I regret our evening of cheap indulgence as the early morning bus jolts down the mountains, switchbacking through the the forests toward the beaches of Nha Trang.

The hangover is bad enough. My concern about my eye infection is worse. I've given up on the pain of wearing my contact lenses and put on my glasses, a pair I bought in the sixties and normally wear only for late-night reading in bed. They're huge round frames with the sort of lenses unflatteringly referred to as Coke bottles, so thick that the glass extrudes well beyond the edges of the frames. With this set of goggles on my face, I feel alien and ugly, divorced from my usual concept of myself. I retreat into a kind of passivity. It's as if whatever happens is not really happening to me. I'm not fully present, not identifying with the woman in those massive tortoise shell circles, her eyes distorted by the lenses' magnification. My real existence is in storage, waiting for my eye to heal.

August 10, Nha Trang

I love this heat and the sultry breeze drifting into our hotel room from the China Sea that lies just across the boulevard. I try to block out the vision of the AIDS billboard set in the boulevard's meridian: big black and white scary Halloween figures gripping a giant hypodermic needle representing the evils of drugs. On posters in Vietnam, sex is not publically admitted as having a role in this disease. But tonight I don't want to deal with the plagues that can confront us, don't want to confront the evils of disease, not even the evils festering in my right eye. I want to indulge myself in heat and the pleasures of mosquito nets.

I love mosquito nets. I love lying back inside them in this bed, swinging out the wooden arms attached to the headboard above me that hold these folds of tightly woven lace. I feel like a princess in a fairy tale, rosy-cheeked and under the spell of some envious stepmother, a spell more profound than the depths of Valium. Just before I succumbed to sleep, I was alert enough to examine this lace for holes. There were plenty. I got out my sewing kit. I stitched. I can fall asleep now, sure that the whines at my ears are only notes, a song that can't penetrate my dreams or skin.

August 11, Nha Trang

I'm addicted to beaches. And in Nha Trang, getting my fix is easy. The morning sea is a delicate pale green, so translucent that my limbs glow under its warm gentle surface. I lie back in the waves, surveying the expanse of water, the blue-tinged mountain ridges in the distance, the palm leaves between me and the town. Morning is the best time to swim here; by afternoon, the sea turns opaque, garbage from the boats drifts in. But I'm a devotee. I spend all day under this sun, alternating between my book and sojourns into the waves. As a veteran of Mexican beaches, I'm accustomed to fending off the local vendors with their load of t-shirts, woven baskets, and jewelery. But here, the things to be sold take a new twist. Women in gaily patterned shirts pass by, with matching cotton pants that always seem a tad too short, their hems ending just above the ankle. They offer massages and manicures, as well as an ingenious method of depilation, to relieve the tourists of offensive leg hairs. Because I'm an old hippie and haven't bothered to shave my legs in years, I constitute a prime target for these women who offer to demonstrate the efficacy of their technique, a method based on the rapid manipulation of a thin string like dental floss that encircles and then plucks the hairs. I refuse their help, but watch them operate on another tourist, their fingers moving nimbly down the leg, leaving behind a pristine shin.

They cluster about a tall American male who constantly banters with them, always buying something: a massage, a lunch of fresh crab. This afternoon, he offers to buy massages for Lana and me. And so we inherit the women who attend him—Mai and her daughter Phuong. Phuong mostly smiles and watches the sea or the local boys. Mai is more intent on addressing us, and sharing the stories of her life that she recounts in such confusing English that I'm never quite sure what to make of them. "Before the real war started," she says, "I helped an American man save his money. I told him, 'get up, your money's being stolen, goddam it, you cowboy, fuck you.'" She explains that she didn't know then what kind of language she was using. It was just the kind of talk she'd heard. The narrative line of her stories meanders; I can't keep the characters and situations straight. When she speaks of all the Western men she knew— "they loved me"—I can't determine whether she means love or simply sex. The only thing that's clear is her poverty and desperation. "They offered to buy me jewels. I was young and stupid and just hungry. I wanted a meal; mostly I loved peanut butter." All of them offered to marry her, she says, to take her to the States, but she didn't want to go. "Why not?" I ask. "I don't know," she says. "I didn't know anything then. I was so young." I have the sense that she was afraid to go, afraid that she'd never be able to come back. And then all those opportunities faded, and the Vietnamese lover that she married died young, and now she sells massages on the beach. And from time to time, the police chase her and the other vendors off. What I understand most clearly from her stories is her tone, its sense of urgency.

I watch these thin, muscled women in brightly flowered pajamas as they lean so freely over the bodies of bantering American males to administer the bargained-for massage. Something in their posture, the ease with which they let their limbs make contact with their customers reminds me of the movements of lovers, and it turns my stomach, as if they'd lost their sense of personal space and dignity. As if they were no longer individuals capable of making a choice to engage joyfully and willingly in the motions of love, but a people who'd grown up in an atmosphere of concubinage, where intimacy was something to sell in return for foreign currency, for refuge and enough to pay a sick grandmother's hospital bills. I suspect that Mai's stories are not unique. I suspect that many woman of her age here could tell the same tale. So what can I do about it now? I go back to my hotel, retrieve a pink cotton shirt, offer it to Mai's daughter as a gift. It's a meager substitute for apology.

August 12, Nha Trang

Last night, I thought a moth had been caught in one of the empty Coca-cola bottles on our room's table. The straw protruding from the bottle was whirling crazily about. I looked inside and saw two pairs of eyes. It was a tiny couple of geckos trapped in the bottle. I up-ended the lizards into the freedom of the pond behind our hotel room where the bats swarmed through a maze of morning glory vines.

This morning, my hysteria equals the wild gyrations of those trapped gheckos. My eye's infection has become a crisis. The inner membranes have turned a swollen purple; huge flecks of disease float past my retina, obscuring my vision. I consult the health section of the guide book. Trachoma, it says, is a common eye infection that can damage your vision if left untreated. I curl up in fetal position on my bed, afraid I'll never again be able to wear my contacts, afraid of entrusting my eye to the care of a doctor whose language I can't understand, and most of all, terrorized that I might lose even the faulty myopic vision of this eye.

I'm still sobbing when Lana returns from breakfast. "If your eye's not better by tomorrow," she says in her most studiedly calming voice, "then we'll call the States, ask your doctor for advice. But I think you should just keep swimming, let the salt waters heal your eye."

I'm ready to grasp at any straw like a trapped gecko. Okay, the sea will heal me. And maybe because I'm in a foreign country, this sort of reassuring talk manages to calm me. Removed from the usual resources I'd use to take control of the situation, I'm more open to trusting in alternative solutions. Plus, the sheer novelty of my surroundings helps distract me from the problem. There are unfamiliar sights to take in while my eyes still have the power to do that. Based on this reasoning, we decide that before we go to test the healing powers of the beach, we'll visit temples. We cross the bridge that leads us past a group of teenagers playing netless volleyball onto the grounds where a cluster of ancient Cham temples still stands, hauntingly organic forms built by people migrating here from India. Their site commands a view of the river, the boats, the green hills in the distance, and closer up, the noisy chaos of the town itself. An entrepreneurial boy with a stack of postcards dogs our heels; on the benches, some women in traditional dress who are probably supposed to serve as guides are heavily involved in gossip. We're glad to escape the services of guides so easily; we enter the first temple, passing into the semi-dark that marks the interior off from the intensity of daytime sun. On the altar, there's the statue of a goddess. I pick up a stick of incense and light it, praying for her blessings to be showered on my eye.

Each of these temples is tiny, built of now-eroded stones with greenery entrenched in the cracks. The temples are outflanked by the stalls of souvenir vendors. I'm just about to refuse the wooden lacquered vase that a woman is handing me when she explains the meaning of the figures that adorn it, each a willowy female similarly dressed but with significantly different styles of hats. "This, Miss Saigon," she says, "and this, Miss Hue and this, Miss Hanoi." I'm a sucker for that kind of symbolism, even though she could be making it up on the spot. I buy vases for myself and friends and family. Back in the States, I'll bring a vase to class and learn from a Vietnamese student that the vendor was honest. The women do, indeed, represent the cities, and it's the style of hat that identifies each one.

The last of the temples features the lingam, the sacred penis. Outside it sits an old man, pretending not to beg. We pretend that we're not handing him money. It's all a matter of saving face.

The Cham temples seem unassuming, blend into the natural landscape. The giant buddha on the other side of the river seems their opposite—a monument to religious civic pride, the product of some local boosterism like those places in the States that tout the world's largest concrete buffalo or a towering statue of Paul Bunyan and his blue ox Babe. This particularly oversized concrete buddha makes a useful landmark, something you can see from wherever you find yourself in the town, and take your bearings. Once you climb the many steps leading up to it, the place offers generous views. The irony is that once you're in a position to enjoy the views, you can't really see the buddha. It's too close to be more than a massive fold of robe.

On the way back to our hotel, we take a wrong turn and end up beside a closed-down Buddhist temple where some skinny vicious dogs bark until we find the local monk who opens the ancient wooden carved door, ushering us in to a world of ruined altars, murals and dust. A neighorhood family gathers at the entrance. On our way out, the monk motions for me to fold my hands and bow to the altar. When I do, the mother in the family grabs my hand, touches it to the nearly hairless skull of her toddler that is covered with horrible red and blue knobs. The child bursts into tears but the mother seems delighted, pleased with the foreigner's blessing, some touch that she believes must hold a blessing and a cure.

I'm not an exemplary healer. I'm afraid of the dogs still baring their fangs in the temple's yard, afraid of adding some infection from those unhealthy ridges on the child's head to the infection raging in my right eye. I can't wait to find a faucet or a fountain where I can wash my hands. I would never make it as some missionary or Florence Nightingale administering to the needs of lepers.

For the rest of the day, I focus selfishly on myself, letting the salt waves wash my eye, the sun penetrate my bones. Then, at dinner, we encounter a male Florence Nightingale at a restaurant ringed by beggars where the waiters rush between the outdoor tables at a pace that belies the climate's heat, a temperature intensified by the restaurant's specialty which involves the placement of a hot pot on the table still bubbling from the coals that sauteed its load of beef or fish. We share a table with a Frenchman named Denis, whose handsomeness makes me periodically take off my thick-lensed glasses, hoping he'll get the idea, hoping he'll realize that I'm just suffering from an eye infection, and normally I'm not this ugly. It's hard to say whether he notices. I'm a vain woman, and he's a useful missionary, a doctor intent on a medical, not religious, conversion of this country. He pays more attention to the problems of the one-legged beggars surrounding the entrance to the restaurant. And rightly so. Somewhere in the pack of them, he thinks he'll find his half-brother, a boy who was about to be sent to France when the U.S. phase of the war intensified, and then in its sudden, inglorious end the helicopters lifted off, carrying only the native Westerners, and his Vietnamese-born brother was left behind, a child already maimed by the bombs. Every one-legged man he meets could share his blood.

After a search of nearly twenty years, Denis has come across a lame beggar whose name almost matches that of his half-brother. He knows that this is not really his relative, but he has informally adopted him anyway. Last week, Denis went into the hills and bought some hand-made crafts from artisans in a village peopled mostly by minorities. "Look," he told the beggar, "you can sell these things to tourists, make a real living." The beggar was shy, reluctant to approach the tourists. Finally, on the sly, Denis collared an American visitor, talked her into buying something. As a result, the lamed man pocketed ten dollars in profit, and his life changed. Now, he has no time for making small talk with Denis; when he surfaces with the crowd of beggars at the restaurant, he's strictly an entrepreneur, self-importantly announcing that he's heading out tomorrow for the village in the mountains, to gather more goods to sell.

August 13, Nha Trang

I've been a tourist in Vietnam now for over a week, a status that—given the qualifications of media analysts these days—entitles me to assume the mantle of an expert, to expound like any news pundit on generalizations about the country. This morning, I'm choosing the topic of gender roles; I'm calling it "divisions of labor." Here's how my analysis goes: Vietnamese women work. Vietnamese men drive. The women sit behind straw baskets of rosy-petaled dragon fruit, baskets of dried shrimp, and stacks of black or white rice pancakes that they fry into a crispy layer above a pot of steaming coals. They do business in the market. The men sit behind the wheels of trucks and buses, motorbikes and cyclos. Sometimes, the men sprawl beside their various vehicles in the scanty bits of shade, smoking the local brand—or better yet, Marlboros or Ho Chi Minh's favorite 555. Some of the women smoke too, but only the old ones, quick-stepping down the streets with a heavy load suspended from their shoulder poles and a hand-rolled cigarette between their lips, fat as a Cuban stogie or a generous joint from the sixties.

Beneath the countryside's unrelenting sun, the women bend across rice paddies, their bare feet sunk deep in the mud and water, tending the green shoots of plants. The men drive past. In the cities, women shovel sand and gravel into baskets, carry those on shoulder poles, building roads and homes. Men drive. Or they wait to drive, lounging in the seats of cyclos, massing on their motorbikes beside a tourist hotel or a bus stop.

Rural or urban, this is how the roles stack up. Men drive. Women do everything else. They scrub the laundry in a river, wash the dishes there and haul them home to chop a fresh-plucked chicken or a fresh-picked mound of greens and stew those over a fire. They add some pink-veined shrimp and a white mess of noodles. This is lunch or dinner or breakfast. The men stop driving then. They eat.

Okay, I'm going a little overboard. I know all about the falsity and faultiness of generalizations. But I can't help making them, can't help succumbing to their elements of truth. Women in this country work. Men, when they are not driving or smoking or eating, piss. Anywhere in the world, even from a distance, the stance of a man pissing is unmistakeable, like this man in a rice field, his feet planted wide apart among the seedlings, his back straight, his vertebrae as vertical as the bones of Cortez in that John Keats' poem about that conquerer from the old world of Europe, standing silent on a peak in Darien, gazing into the new world. This man I'm watching in the fields is surveying the yellow arc of his own stream steaming into some place, either new or old, the pot that men seem to think they fill with gold. The stance has nothing to do with being Vietnamese; it has everything to do with being male. Mostly, these men are pissing into some body of water—a river behind the market, a lake, the sudden swell created by a typhoon rain above a clogged storm drain. But anything will do: a wall, a field, the green expanse of an old world or a new one.

Perhaps my comments seem unfair. Driving is, after all, a difficult job on pot-holed roads—and a perilous one, given the chaos of traffic and its flirtation with head-on collisions. The men must suffer from stress; no wonder they need to relieve themselves so often in public. I admit that my attempts at sympathy sound fake, even to my own ears. After all, half of the stress arises simply from the way these men drive; the other half is the stress that I'm suffering which stems from the men's love of horns, their fingers tapping them like a drummer with an obsessive tic. On really bad days, I've considered shipping all the men to some isolate spot in Antarctica.

On more generous days, I envision taking a leaf from the models of hard-line regimes and establishing re-education camps for those men with a potential for reform—for learning to hold up their half of the sky and to do that more quietly. For entrance to the camps, I'll devise a triage test. Any male who can keep his fingers off a car's horn for more than sixty seconds will pass. I do not anticipate many graduates.

But to tell the real truth, I'm wary of generalizations. Stretched too far, they're like bubble gum, they develop holes. In my litany of gender generalizations, I make an exception for the cyclo drivers, men with muscled calves that peddle loads of heavy foreigners with luggage, peddle mattresses and couches, twenty cases of Coke in bottles. This afternoon, I had a long talk with one of the Vietnamese women who offer manicures and massages on the beach. A typically thin woman— all wiry bones and labor. She has worked hard, and works harder now that her husband has died, leaving her to support three children and an ailing mother. When they met, the woman said, her husband was the chauffeur of some official's private car. Because of that, he always had a lot of flirtatious women hanging around him. When he asked her to marry him, he promised to give up being a chauffeur, to forego the admiring women. He became a cyclo driver. He died young. His heart gave out. It's a hard job, the woman told me, peddling those loads on bikes.

1970, Bombing Cambodia

In politics, I was never a leader, but sometimes I fell into it by default—and still do. In 1970, I was quoted by the university student newspaper as a spokesperson for the demonstration just because I happened to be there and the reporter happened to pick me to interview. And last week, I ended up speaking for my neighborhood's demonstration against Bush junior's war on Iraq simply because the true neighborhood organizer gave my name and number to the local news editor.

Inadvertently, I fell into leadership at an English department meeting when the students at the University of Washington were protesting the U.S. bombing of Cambodia—an auxiliary to the nation's war on Vietnam. It was the first time the department had allowed graduate students to attend a department meeting. I raised my hand to make a motion that we cancel classes in sympathy with student protests. Maybe it's only a figment of my current middle-aged memory, but I recall that the department chair recognized me as "the little lady in the ruffled blouse." Even if that memory is apocryphal, it's accurate—those were the days I wore long skirts, elegant blouses, lots of draping scarves or shawls and the patchouli oil that the department chair confused with the scent of pot.

In any case, my motion got made and somebody seconded it, and then it was truth and consequences time: department members had to vote by a show of hands, for or against canceling classes in protest of the war. My motion failed, but afterwards in the elevator, a real faculty member—as opposed to my graduate student status—thanked me for taking the risk of making that motion. I responded with a quote from a Bob Dylan tune, "If you ain't got nothin,' you got nothin' to lose." Never again did the department invite graduate students to a meeting.

Nha Trang, August 14

Lana and I check out of our hotel and check onto Mama Hanh's boat tour. Of all the day trips leaving the harbor to explore the nearby islands, we've heard that this is the best, but the beginning of it leaves us feeling dubious. We've made it past the hour of standing around in the hot sun, attacked by crowds of ten-year-old water sellers who hold their iced wares against our skin—a sales tactic we particularly welcome even though we're already carrying plenty of bottled water and don't intend to buy. But now so many of us tourists have crowded onto the boat's two levels that it's sunk too deep, and we seem to be permanently grounded on the harbor's rocks. While a ferry beside us fills with locals sucking colored ice on sticks, the crew commands us to cluster at the back of the boat, to take the weight off the rocks in front. Still, nothing happens. Finally, the boats on either side of us pull away, their engines straining at ropes attached to our own pleasure craft, and we're off the shoals and at sea.

I lean over the bow, snapping photos of the large rusty hulls anchored near the port, documents to convince my friends back home that this truly is a working harbor. But really this is a tourist venture, and once we're sufficiently underway, we drop anchor again, for a morning of swimming and snorkeling. Mama Hanh, a diminutive woman in shorts with a business-like manner softened by a sense of humor huddles in the tiny closet-sized galley with two assistants, turning a stash of fresh fish and vegetables into a feast. We head into a cove beside a settlement of wooden houses on an island, and everybody climbs to the top deck which is spread with dishes: shelled crab, calamari drenched in herbs, marinated potatoes, unnamed vegetables in equally unnamed but delicious sauces. We dig in with chopsticks and fingers; morsels of food roll about on the deck, but we spear them anyway, oblivious to the dictates of sanitation. The crew keep passing cans of soda pop and beer; a lot of it spills, some of it runs beneath the bits of deck we've perched on, saturating our bathing suits with the scent of malt and hops, the stickiness of Coca-cola. Just when we think our appetites are sated, the boat sets sail for another island and drops anchor fifty feet from the shore. Standing in the shallow waves, we tourists form a line like a fire brigade, passing china plates filled with fruit from hand to hand until they arrive at the plastic tables the crew has set up on the beach: dragon fruit, kiwis, apples, giant grapefruit, slices of oranges, bananas, bunches of grapes. More than a congregation twenty times our size could consume. The last item to hand over is the cassette player with a car battery to fuel it so our banquet is accompanied by the sounds of a Cat Stevens tape. Mama Hanh sits on the sand beside the last table, picking miniscule snails from a bucket, using a toothpick to pry the occupants from their shells, then swallowing them raw.

To believe that this is Vietnam seems impossible. There's no blast of bombs, no helicopter drone. Only Cat Stevens. There are no napalm-enflamed bodies. Only the anorexic French tourist who's making a show of removing her bikini top to let her shoulders and spine be greased with sunblock, a protection she's applying far too late. To say that her back is lobster red is understatement. Although already cooked, she resembles flayed rare beef.

Our last stop is an island fishing village. In economic terms, the village seems a mass of contradictions: a shoreline of dire poverty and direr sanitation backed by an incongruous mix of hovels and prosperous homes with finely carved doors opening onto halls of sumptuous terracotta decor. But the overall resourcefulness of the place reminds me of the futility of generals who think that sophisticated technology assures they'll win the war. We tie up to a set of floating rafts under-slung with nets where the residents snare countless fish and crabs, including the horseshoe crab that they're exhibiting now, one of the oldest species still on earth. The efficiency of that fishing system is matched by an ingenious system that ferries us ashore. There's a rope strung between our boat and a pole on the beach; we step onto a raft and a small boy reaches hand over hand along the rope, pulling us in. The simplicity of it undermines the millions that my country spends on Stealth bombers.

Mama Hanh's tour deposits us back at the harbor of Nha Trang, where Lana and I wander the beaches till we find a public shower where we can wash off the worst of the sand and salt before we board the train to Danang. We have tickets for a "soft berth" which we find is a compartment of four hard bunks supplied with a sheet and a pillow—a space like the cages in a zoo with metal grilles over the windows. There's a fan that functions erratically, but a cooling wind roars steadily in all night with its load of grime and soot, while the rails maintain a noisy percussion. At dawn, we make our first stop, and the vendors on the tracks below us set up a chant in various accents, announcing coffee, cafee, cafe. I've rolled up the metal bars across our window, tied them with a string that apparently some other occupants have similarly employed. Now the vendors' hands stretch through the window. A train attendant enters and scolds me; she unfastens the bars, sets them back in place. I guess that "soft berth" simply refers to stratagems for keeping the riff-raff at bay. But her system of bars also shuts out the landscape. As soon as she leaves, I draw the bars up, spend the morning watching the passage of rice fields and water buffaloes, conical stacks of hay, and the teamwork of pairs of peasants—each holding the end of a rope from which a bucket dangles. Rhythmically they dip the bucket in the irrigation ditches, then swing its load of water toward the fields.

I'm so hungry that I actually devour the lifeless soft slices (reminiscent of Wonder Bread) in the breakfast box delivered by our train attendant, along with the tasteless gooey cheese wrapped in silver foil emblazoned with the picture of a smiling cow. The breeze that attacks our windows has learned nothing from Marxist philosophies about equality. On Lana's side of our cage, the wind whips through the train window, filling her pores with grit, a blast not only cooling but unpleasant, strong enough to take her breath away. On my side, there's only deadly humid space, nothing stirring.

August 15, Danang

Certain names in Vietnam seem all too familiar. Danang is one of them. A name that conjures up reports of body counts on the nightly news, or tales of military R & R on nearby China Beach. Our guide book notes that some people insist that this isn't the real site of that "rest and relaxation" beach for American enlisted men, that the country is just capitalizing on the notoriety of the place in order to draw tourists to the beach's government-owned hotel, where street vendors specialize in kitsch like baseball caps emblazoned with the China Beach name. Parenthetically, our guide book also notes that in 1992, this beach was the site of the first international surfing competition in Vietnam.

The combination of our memories of Danang's war-time reputation and the guide book's surfer scenario makes a paradoxical introduction to the place. But stepping out of the train station into arguments with cab drivers over fares, we feel no paradox, no ambiguity about the city. There's no suggestion here of blonde muscled surfers singing about the beauty of California girls. It's strictly an evil place, we think. And everything that happens confirms our judgment. We ask the taxi driver to take us to the Hai Van Hotel, but he pulls up in front of another building that he swears is really the same place. "Just new owners," he says. "Just new now." This is obviously not the truth. The hotel is about as new as the sleaze bag dives in porno films. And the taxi driver is clearly on some under-the-counter payroll, encouraged to deliver unwary tourists to the door. We accept the fact that we're at his mercy. We've been deposited, and, after all, it is a place with beds. But we're in no mood to be conned. We refuse to pay him for the ride, pointing out that he refused to take us to the address we gave him. There's some consultation between him and the hotel receptionist. Lana and I stand firm. The driver doesn't insist on his fare. Probably, he'll get his payoff from the hotel anyway.

The receptionist leads us up the flights of stairs to a room fronting the street, with an air conditioner that leaks buckets of water even though we never actually turn it on. Danang stretches below us: loud and hot and dusty and mostly ugly despite the river that would in any other place be termed a redeeming feature. Lana collapses on one of the lumpy beds, while I fill the sink with laundry, tie my skinny clothesline between the bedpost and the doorknob, suspending my soggy nightgown and t-shirts from the doll-sized clothespins in my travel kit. We concentrate on ways to get out of town, berating ourselves for our lack of travel savvy in planning our itinerary. We never wanted to visit Danang or China Beach or the nearby Marble Mountains where we've heard the religious and natural sights are obscured by masses of tourists and equally massive numbers of Vietnamese hawking souvenirs. Really, we wanted to visit Hoi An, a small town just south of here, but the train arrived there at an awkward hour for finding accommodation, and the tourist grapevine had told us that rooms might be scarce. Okay, we'd thought, we'll just base ourselves in Danang, and make a day trip to Hoi An. A bad decision. But travel is like that, a hit and miss operation. Sometimes you gamble wrong. Neither of us is willing to give up the possibility of touring Hoi An. And ever since I saw a magazine photo of the mist-encircled peaks of Hai Van Pass, I've had my heart set on taking that road north from Danang to the city of Hue. So far, as traveling companions, we've found a way to accommodate our separate desires. This time, we're stumped because we're not just compromising with each other, we're compromising with the country, and we're not sure about its travel options.

On the dingy waterfront, in a greasy restaurant with lazily indifferent service, we eat a lunch of fried fish that we worry were probably caught in the murky waters passing beneath our table. Although it's really too early in the day for alcohol, we order beer to fortify us for a trip to the city's tourist office. Once we arrive there, we find that for travelers not on an organized tour, there's not much real choice. We listen to a range of prices that change by the minute, depending on which group of tourists is doing the asking, which clerk is providing the answers. We stand around for at least an hour, passed from one assistant to another, and finally to what seems to be the head man, who assures us that he's booked a room for us in Hue in the hotel that we read about in the travel section of *The New York Times*, a place rumored to be an inexpensive getaway with quiet gardens, a retreat that, up till now, the travel agents have always told us is full. And suddenly, we're agreeing to rent a car and driver to carry us there tomorrow, complete with a side-trip to Hoi An and stopovers in Hai Van Pass—an extravagance we know we've paid too much for, but any price seems acceptable if it gets us quickly out of Danang.

Business concluded, we head aimlessly down the street, and stumble onto the one compelling reason for a sojourn in Danang: a museum so overflowing with bounty from Cham temples that the yard surrounding it is littered with bits of carved stone bodies and faces flung here and there among the grass and trees. The statues that have managed to be preserved inside the museum's walls delight and fascinate me, despite the difficulty of trying to discern their features in the dim, sometimes downright nonexistent natural lighting. The rooms and corridors of the museum teem with sassy lions and surreal sea monsters, Buddhas with their limbs coiled in the serenity of lotus positions, gods in the guise of elephants or birds, phallic lingams surrounded by a frieze of breasts. Everything about the space is simultaneously spiritual and playfully sensual—a combination of emotions I'd never find in a Western religion, and qualities that, outside the province of this museum, are utterly missing from the city of Danang.

August 15, Danang

This is what you do at night when you're lodged in a city you want to escape from, and the laundry's finished, and you've already sewed the missing buttons onto all your clothes. You study the country's language. Normally, I'm more conscientious; normally, I study in the weeks before my plane lifts off, getting out the grammar books to review my tenuous command of French or Spanish or Chinese, spending hours at the university's library, watching videos in the target language. But this time, I admit, I was lazy. I'm only going on a month's vacation, I rationalized. Even after a year in China, I never really got the tones right; how could I expect to function in Vietnamese? And why bother, I thought, expecting that my French would get me by, thanks to the holdovers from colonization, and English would function as the new colonizing language. Being ill at ease with the role of colonizer, I did try to learn some Vietnamese before I left home, but all the language books I consulted were less than satisfactory in giving me a useful roadmap to the rules of pronunciation. Actually, I got my best clues from watching a Vietnamese karaoke video one night in a sushi restaurant. But I'm determined not to be the sort of ugly American who expects the world to function in perfect English. I picked up a few words from my guide book, a few more from the cyclo driver in Ho Chi Minh City, enough to cause a sensation among the young women vendors in the cavernous central market. They were selling baseball caps of tie-dyed silk patterns, with long sashes suspended from the caps to knot into a bow. I liked the caps; in my halting Vietnamese, I indicated that I'd like to buy not just one, but three of them, as presents for myself and friends. The teenaged saleswomen in their flowered pajama blouses and pants and their long black ponytails kept bursting into giggles. I was never sure whether they were laughing at my pronunciation or simply the fact that I was trying to speak their language. Or maybe they were just amused at the number of hats that I was buying.

This afternoon, when the postcard-selling children clamored around us, I noticed one whose cache of goods included a book entitled *How*

To Speak Vietnamese. The book was tiny, a paperback about the size of those pocket novels once designed for enlisted men to carry into the trenches. It wouldn't constitute a significant extra burden in the luggage that, so far, I'd kept scaled down to one nylon shoulder bag.

Now, trying to decipher the print beneath the hotel's dim lamp, I'm glad I made this purchase. Not because it will help me speak Vietnamese. It will clearly never do that. But as a source of amusement, it's worth every bit of dong I paid. "A rapid mastery of the Vietnamese," the subtitle proclaims. And it's certainly that—a phrasebook of the sorts of things the snobby colonizers might have said, as they went about assuring their sovereignty over the country. Being practical, I turn first to the section on Hygiene and Health; I find translations for such life-threatening situations as "I want a shave. I want my hair cut. Just trim around the back and ears. Your blade scratches. Put a little powder, some eau de Cologne. Give me a hot towel. I don't want brillantine." The ladies are equally demanding: "Trim my eyebrows. Part my hair in the middle. (I'd like) bobbed shingled hair. Shall I have to wait long?" The subheading called "at the doctor's" offers me nothing but the parenthetical reference "See also 'How are you?'"

I move on to matters perhaps more important than hygiene. In the section on clothing, I find that the language student must choose among a variety of situations: at the tailor's, at the dressmaker's, at the shirt maker's, at the linen draper's, at the hatter's, at the milliner's, at the laundress's, at the haberdasher's, at the hosier's, and at the shoemaker's. Then follows a section entitled Shopping, beginning with advice for being "at the stores." Apparently, the other more-specialized clothing outlets are considered a cut above something so commonplace as "stores," and in them, one does not simply buy, one demands. At least that's the attitude reflected in the phrases the author has chosen to translate: "I want a frock coat, a lounge coat, a dinner jacket. Show me some light stuffs, dark stuffs, of excellent quality, pure wool. It's too expensive. Must I make a deposit? There is a crease at the back. The collar doesn't fall right. Have you got anything better? I should want it for Saturday. Don't starch the linen too much. This boot is too tight. They pinch at the toes. Don't put this in the washing tub. Try and remove this stain. I shall want this for Monday. How much will you charge?"

Obviously, I'll never find a phrase in this book that I could imagine myself uttering. Still, I persevere, turning to the chapter entitled Public Notices. The first entry is "men," followed by "genltemen" (spelled just like that), then "ladies," then "entrance, way in," "exit, way out," "danger," stairs," "lift, elevator." At this point, I think I'm in the midst of instructions pertaining to a natural disaster. But the litany ends with a series of words that seem more useful for engaging in some sort of slightly crooked lottery: "fixed price," "ticket," booking-office." The blunt brevity of the public notice entries is counterbalanced by the formality in the chapter devoted to Commercial Phrases: "We shall be pleased to receive your further orders which shall always have our best attention." "The firm about whom you inquire has only a very small account with us." "This information is given in strict confidence and without any responsibility on our part." "We are sending you here with invoice in triplicate, consular invoice in duplicate."

By the time I've perused the food section, with its terms for cruet stands, soup tureens, pheasant, partridge, wood cock, thrush, and fat pullet, I'm thumbing back to the title page, checking to see what nineteenth-century Englishman compiled this book's list of necessary phrases. 1992 reads the publication date, above an authentically Vietnamese author's name. In the country's history, I don't recall any periods of British colonization. Maybe the British were simply the first to offer courses in English as a foreign language, and the author grew up on a surfeit of William Thackeray. I can't imagine the processes of this man's mind, deciding to fill his pages with the Vietnamese terms for silk chemises and Havana cigars. I can't believe that such terms exist in the language spoken by the men peddling cyclos and the women stirring vats of noodles. Still, in the preface to the book, the author swears that "a careful study of these short talks, all of immediate application, will moreover prove the best of all direct methods." As a kind of caveat, he adds, "the best thing is to get a Vietnamese to help you listen carefully! Imitate his pronunciation and practice until he is satisfied."

Abandoning all hope of language learning, I decide to treat the book as a soporific; I'll read myself to sleep. Tomorrow, we're setting off early with our rented car and driver, so I turn to the pages entitled Travelling, subheading "on the road by car." The succession of entries there makes me feel that I've curled up with a mystery novel in which the primary suspect carries an arsenal of alibis: "Your lights are not on. Your number cannot be seen. You drive too fast. You have damaged my car. You were not keeping to your right. It was my road. I tried to avoid that carriage. I tried to avoid that cyclist. I tried to avoid an infant. I was dazzled by your lights. You did not blow your horn. I had to apply the brake all at once. I skidded on the wet ground." After this spate of attempts to wriggle out of what is clearly a complicated plot, the suspect turns on the accusers: "Give me your names and address, the name of your insurance company, your place and date of birth. Call for a doctor at once. Can you oblige me by helping me to get out this? I've had a breakdown." I leap out of bed for a pen and some paper. At last I've found a truly useful phrase, one I can utter at least once a day. Carefully I copy the Vietnamese for "I've had a breakdown"—xe toi bi hong. I picture myself standing before the bank clerk who has just refused to cash my travelers checks because I've neglected to carry the receipts, or the travel agent who keeps serving other tourists while she puts my requests on hold. In my fantasy, I pass my hand delicately across my brow and weakly whisper "Xe toi bi hong," the prelude to a nineteenth-century heroine's fictional faint. I hope the phrase is as generic in Vietnamese as it is in English where the speaker can break down in so many ways. I hope there's no mechanical connotation embedded in the language, causing my audience to wonder why I'm announcing the condition of my overheated radiator, my broken axle, my inexplicably flat tire.

August 16,
In Our Rented Car with Our Equally Rented Chauffeur

For the first time, we've splurged, commissioned a private car that will carry us south to Hoi An, then north to Hue. We're newcomers to this high-priced version of travel and almost let its rewards escape us, accustomed to the passivity of passengers on a bus who know it's futile to ask the driver to make a detour. Passing the outskirts of Danang, we spot a temple site, and deliberate so long we almost miss the opportunity to ask the driver to stop, to throw the engine into reverse and let us visit.

Just in time, we find the right degree of assertiveness. And then we're clambering down a weed-obstructed hill to a sort of path through fields behind homes, a route that takes us to a clearing dominated by the recent architectural fantasies of temple designers. Disney surfaces again. This is a Buddhist Disneyland, with the central temple shrine surrounded by giant dragons, griffins, and other mythic creatures constructed of bits of stone, colored glass, and shards of porcelain plates. The beasts' magnificent jaws yawn above the concrete-covered square; they lift their heads and paws from pedestals backed by a three-storied condominum for birds, flanked by green-foliaged cliff. The mosaic decor seems more like fanciful kitsch than a testament to spirituality; the pastoral setting itself seems to supply that spiritual aspect, with real birds calling in the trees to mimic the manufactured animals, with an expanse of wild grasses leading away from the aesthetic busyness of the site itself toward the fields where a bevy of local children coalesce and then follow us back up the rudimentary trail to our car.

And then we're on our way to Hoi An, a village that in earlier centuries was an international port of call. Ironically, its fame arises now partly from the fact that it's the most Chinese-like town in Vietnam. I say "ironically" because the history of Vietnam includes so much domination by China and its armies that Ho Chi Minh himself once said of his decision to make a pragmatically political pact with his European colonizers, "I'd rather smell French shit for five years than Chinese shit forever." Since I've never been dominated by China, only subject to periods of nostalgia for the country ever since the year that I lived there, I'm captivated by the "China-ness" of Hoi An, a quality that now resides mostly in its architecture, the curved up-swing of tiled roofs. But the Chinese communities have also left their mark on the town's religious sites such as the Fujian temple with a shrine to the protectress of the sea, a doll-sized figure inside a glass-fronted case with a red lacquered frame, surrounded by her sidekicks who are said to be able to hear and see for a thousand miles. Beside the altar of the protectress, there's a miniature boat, and a picture portraying big waves engulfing a similar craft, and the miracle of everyone saved. Outside the entrance to another tiny shrine, beer cans frame the door, bearing the brand name 333—in the Vietnamese language, the numbers of that name translate as "ba ba ba," a lilting request Lana and I delight in making in restaurants.

Hoi An now is fodder for tourists. As we walk the streets between the designated sites, we stop to consult the guide book in front of a yet another sacred building. A woman vending sweets outside it shouts "Number 13 on the map." So far, for foreigners, there is only one map to Vietnam, the one provided in the Lonely Planet guide book. Apparently, the townsfolk have memorized it. Normally, I'd disapprove of monopolies, but I appreciate the Lonely Planet's reassuring stranglehold on foreign tourism. It will be so much more difficult to get my bearings when the competition arrives.

Already, there's a competition to prove who occupies the oldest, most historic house. To our innocent, unpracticed eyes, all of them seem old, constructed inside and out of the finest woods, weathered now—sanctuaries offering coolness in summer, warmth in winter. We enter one that bears the blessing of the historical society and find altars with pictures of the great-grandparents who once legitimately lived here among the massive mahogany beams inlaid with poems constructed in bits of mother of pearl, the shells arranged so that the characters or letters of the words resemble birds and butterflies lifting their wings. Behind this grandeur, there's the simplicity of the current family's actual living quarters. A daughter arrives with a tray of tea cups, earnestly repeating the information that she hands us on a photocopied sheet, smiling as we drop our donation into the glass vase on her tray.

Down the street, small shops offer lovely silk blouses and jackets only in size extra large (apparently the one-size-fits-all of foreigners). The window of a store catering to locals features a prom gown with pink crinoline skirts, a black and silver girdle around the waist and a red fake feather bodice. On the wall beside the gown, a calendar portrait of a Western beauty in a deshabille off-the-shoulder bit of silk keeps watch. To our right lies the river where fishermen string burgundy-colored nets on poles, like the inverted canopies of four-poster beds. A girl in a flowered yellow shirt and matching shorts turns a wheel of long spikes connected to a four-legged blue contraption that grinds the stalks of sugar cane into a pulp that can be mixed with water and sold as a refreshing drink. But this is a delicacy for the natives, not the tourists. Everybody knows the habits of foreigners, knows their chief requirement; on every corner, signs announce "Coke, beer, mineral water, COLD."

Not everything that's famous about Hoi An has to do with history. There's a local culinary speciality called cao lau that we want to sample for lunch. We've seen signs for it everywhere, as part of the eclectic pitch aimed at tourist palates: "Cao lau, banana pancakes, french fries." In a cafe noted for this dish, the waiters bring us first some bread with a pork pâté, then banana leaves wrapped around bits of pork, and sweet bean cakes enfolded in packages of more banana leaves. Then the cao lau itself arrives: flat noodles mixed with croutons, bean sprouts, and greens, topped by slices of pork. The ingredients don't seem particularly unique, but our guide book assures us that it's the water in the broth that really counts. Only a specific well in the town can supply the water for a genuine cao lau.

Already, it's mid-afternoon, and we have to reach Hue by sunset in order for our driver to return home. We find him asleep beside the park that rims the town hall. Back on the highway, we learn that, as usual, progress is never the straight line that we've assumed. Our route takes us through the driver's village where the gross national product focuses on the manufacture of fireworks. Instead of the baskets of potted flowers that aesthetically-minded cities back home suspend from lamp posts—a detail calculated to entice the tourists—here, in this village, the light posts are hung with decorative boxes filled with fireworks for sale. We stop at one home to admire the handiwork of children sitting cross-legged beside woven baskets housing mountains of yellow powder and a row of fuses. In my photo of the scene, each child stares solemnly into the lens, their skinny arms folded at the elbows, resting their chins and fists on the sticks they apparently use to stuff the fuses. Like them, I take my fireworks seriously; I'm a pyromanic at heart, a devotee of loud, sparkling conflagrations. At home, where my city has outlawed fireworks, I make pilgrimages to the reservations where Native Americans own the right to sell such flimsy bursts of color and noise; I husband my cache in a drawer—this much to be exploded on my birthday, this much for the Chinese New Year, this much for the Fourth of July. When I lived in China—the country that invented fireworks, I once shinnied up the flagpole on the grounds of a hotel complex in order to light the fuse of a firework that opened a cage where a paper bird sang. Our circle of foreign friends set off a lot of fireworks that night, while a Chinese guard stood at the edge, vaguely smiling. The next day, we learned that a visiting dignitary was housed in the hotel; his bodyguards had been on the verge of declaring our blasts to be the sound of enemy gunfire or grenades. For some reason, the Chinese guard had neglected to inform us of this situation. For some miraculous reason, the bodyguards hadn't retaliated. That narrow escape hasn't taught me any lessons. I lust after the plastic bags of assorted pyrotechnics that line this Vietnamese street of vendors. Only the difficulty of smuggling them through U.S. customs keeps me from filling my bags with these heavenly bursts of flamboyant contraband.

August 16, Hai Van Pass

This passage is so spectacular that it seems to demand a journal entry all to itself. It begins with the grinding effort of a steep climb past the buses and trucks that have already broken down. The steepness of the grade exhausts even the resourcefulness of truck drivers who have learned to deal with the shortage of parts that stems from the U.S. ban on trade, drivers who have long ago abandoned the hope of replacing their broken radiators and simply positioned a barrel on the top of their truck's cab, letting the fall of gravity carry water down a hose connecting that barrel with their engine. At gas stations, there's a special pump for what's called "barrel water." On any road, there's the tell-tale trace of that water spilling behind a truck.

The road climbs into mountains covered with a velvety layer of green, peaks rising above the sea that's studded with peninsulas and islands. On the slopes between the views, lie farmed lands. At various switchback curves on the ascent, lie so-called stores, little more than a thatched roof stacked on a few worn studs, with a motorbike parked in front, a shack vending the barest of essentials. We stop over and over for photos of the banks of mist and the repeating lines of jagged ridges that stretch below us, each slope lusciously dense with vegetation. Hai means sea; van means clouds; the pass is more than appropriately named. In some weathers, the atmosphere's too thick to see even a meter ahead; those are the days that the trucks give up on the ascent and turn around. This afternoon, I watch pillars of black smoke, thinking that the forests must be on fire; I learn it's only the diesel smoke from the trucks in a country where fuel can be very cheap, costing as little as twenty-five cents a liter, because the exploration teams have discovered a cache of oil in the sea-port of Vung Tau.

At the top of the pass stand the military ruins of U.S. and French ramparts, along with a religious shrine, and hordes of vendors—mostly girls who are students at an English school and have actually ridden their bikes up the steep miles from Danang. Today has been a bad one for their commercial ventures—hardly any tourists, hardly any sales. I buy a lukewarm Coke from their cooler, happy to support this sort of dedication, this eager pursuit of schooling that seduces them into peddling up these mountains to pay the costs of tuition.

On the descent, we catch sight of Long Co, a long peninsula fronted by the astoundingly white sands of a quiet beach, backed by a tiny town—another place I'd wanted to visit, but hadn't lobbied hard enough to achieve a stopover. Now I wish I'd lied to Lana, wish I'd told her that the streets were lined with temples worth a once-in-a-lifetime visit.

Along the road, the villagers have spread a layer of rice and one of hay that extend toward the mound of yellow and green grain that towers above a man's head. They let the grains dry in the sun, to be threshed by passing wheels. For one last time, I tap the driver on the shoulder, indicating that I want him to stop. The angle of the sunset is firing up the shocks of hay beside the road, and off to the left, in the rolling field with a backdrop of mountains whose peaks disappear into a white tangled billow of clouds, there's a scattered herd of water buffaloes. I snap the photo, and climb back into the car, sure that at last I've captured the country's heart on film, forgetting that my camera has a way of turning any long-distance shot into a frame of tiny dots that only my memory can decipher, a distantly ambiguous exposure that will mean nothing to my friends back home.

August 17, Hue

So much for believing in the travel wisdom of *The New York Times*. Last night, we checked into one of the rooms in the hotel that the paper's travel writer raved about, only to find that our section of the hotel's cottages was under construction, and situated near a bog, a locale that featured the Louisiana gospel bass of frogs in the pond all night, accompanied by the whine of mosquitoes. For hours, the power cut in and out, as heat lightning flashed, and the small refrigerator died with a whir, returned to life with a dream-jarring groan. At dawn, the rhythm of workers' shovels kicked in, accompanied by their chest-dredging spits. "We're out of here somehow," Lana declared, her hand on the doorknob, her big lavendar sunhat set determinedly on her blonde head. And by the time that I had finished fighting with the shower's erratic supply of hot and cold, and was brushing my teeth with bottled water, she was back, announcing that she'd found a place without either frogs or construction, for only $10 a night.

So here we are in the Marin, which years ago used to be a set of horse stables with accommodation for their riders on the second storey—a huge circular bank of rooms arranged around a large courtyard. Our room lies on the horse floor. It's a concrete space, with extremely high ceilings, a damp and cavernous expanse featuring three cots lined up beneath headboards with mosquito netting. Beside the door, a set of instructions is posted: 1. Show legal papers. 2. Don't be noisy. 3. Don't cook, don't iron. 4. When leaving, give room keys to reception, and please put on appropriately.

At the southern end, a wall marks off a small bathroom with a shower whose spray cleanses the entire enclosure and provides a haven for mosquitoes. At the north end, we have three windows that open onto an alley bisected by standing pools of water that breed (you guessed it) more mosquitoes.

But tonight I don't care about the voracious appetites of biting insects. I'm relaxing in the courtyard, drinking slightly lukewarm beer, trying to match my pen to the lines of my writing tablet that the dim overhead lights and the candle on my table hardly illuminate. A storm's brewing up, stirring the heat and some fallen leaves, periodically snuffing my candle. An American woman walks by, wearing a tall crown and a yellow imperial robe covered with embroidery; she's followed by several tourists and hotel waiters, all of them clapping in unison. Earlier, at one of the grand hotels, I saw a sign advertising a Vietnamese version of "Queen for a Day." "Be emperor for the night," the caption read beneath a photo of smiling tourists dressed in ancient court garb. I guess our own rockbottom hotel has its own version of that game, or maybe it's a multicultural sort of event, since just before the storm knocks out the power, I hear them singing "Happy Birthday." Whatever the purpose of these festivities, I'm glad I'm sitting some distance away from them because somebody in the group has lit two long strings of the loudest firecrackers I've ever heard, and for a good five minutes in the power-outage dark, it's the war all over again, and I'm temporarily deafened.

Back at our room, I fumble with the key to the padlock that hinges the pair of swinging stable doors. Lana's already asleep beneath the folds of mosquito netting, with the ceiling fan turning lazily above her. Despite the breeze from the fan, our room's so hot and humid that we lie naked under our mosquito nets. In the middle of the night, some guy in the alley shines his flashlight through the windows. The beam doesn't wake me, but Lana's on the alert, shooing the man away, hanging sheets across the windows. Miraculously, I sleep through this, drugged by the heat and the warm beer.

August 18, Hue

This morning, sitting cross-legged on our cots, using our pocket knives to hack some dragon fruit and the bread saved from dinner into a reasonable breakfast, Lana fills me in on last night's trauma. I feel stupidly vulnerable and violated, wondering how much of my flesh lay exposed beneath the flashlight's beam. But compared to our own country, Vietnam seems comfortingly safe. We don't even consider moving from our hotel; we simply tuck the sheets more securely around the alley windows, sure that what we're dealing with is the prurience of voyeurs—annoying but not threatening—peeping Toms or Nguyens, not robbers or rapists. I feel more confident about entrusting myself to the country's crime rate than to its medical expertise. On a scale of one to ten, I'd rate my concern about the voyeur as a three; I'd say my frets about my constant eye infection have fallen from a twelve to a nine. I no longer wake with my eye completely encrusted. Either the salt waves at Nha Trang or the prayer to its Cham temple goddess have proved beneficial. But my eye remains an angry red; I'm still relegated to wearing the ugliness of my Coke-bottle glasses. Lana's eyesight far surpasses mine. She wears glasses for certain tasks, not for daily navigation through her routine world. She can take them off, and still function. As a result, she's an enthusiast of eye glasses, collecting different fashions the way I collect jewelry or clothes. Already, she's acquired a new pair in Vietnam where the price is only a fraction of that charged in the States. She watches me dump the remains of breakfast into the bathroom wastebasket, then unhappily check my reflection in the cloudy mirror. "Your glasses are not nearly so ugly as you think," she says. "You just feel ugly in them. Why don't you get a new pair today? There must be an optometrist's shop near the market."

She's right. There's a shop just beyond the bridge; we split up, Lana heading toward the market, me wandering into an hour of trying to stand close enough to the mirrors to assess the look of various frames. The optometrist hovers around me, anxious to please. I've narrowed my selection down to two pairs, one of them more satisfying than the other. The optometrist tries to save me from financial disaster. "This one," he says, "made in France. Too expensive. This one come from Hong Kong. Much better." But I feel more beautiful in the frames from France. "How much?" I say, holding up each pair. He points first to the Hong Kong product. "Only seven U.S. dollars." Then the French style. "This, thirty dollars. Most expensive in the shop." At first, I try to explain that the price would be at least five times as much in the States, but this only confuses him. He waves his hands, no, no, no, not that much, thinking I've misunderstood his price. I turn back to the mirror. Yes, the French frames are definitely more flattering. Normally, I'd go for the bargain, but my sense of my face and my ego are at stake—and I can satisfy my vanity for so much less than it would cost at home. I hand him the French frames, and the requisite stack of Vietnamese dong. He takes a reading from my old thick plastic lenses. By five o'clock, my new look will be ready, complete with a beige suede leather case advertising lenses made in Italy. A soundly multicultural bargain.

In the bewildering maze of Hue's blocks of street markets, my bargaining skills are not so astute. Just figuring out where the market begins and ends, and where I am once I've stepped inside it would be victory enough. But as soon as I've turned off the wide busy street into the first of the market's narrow passages, I'm happily lost. Oh, sure, there is a kind of order. The same category of goods is more or less stationed in the same area: shoes in a section so dark that you might buy platform heels and think you'd purchased tennis sneakers; stalls of woven straw baskets—just the size you think you'll need to haul your other purchases home. I squeeze between the crowded aisles featuring hardware, then china dishes, then rows of underpants fashioned either of lace or serviceable cotton, followed by religious paraphernalia including pictures of a goddess that nobody can name. But she appeals to me, smiling benignly above an entourage of elephants. And so I buy her, along with the wooden stand that houses her, its edges cut into a sequence of red-painted curliques. (Later, I'll find that Lana has bought a similar goddess souvenir; she'll take it to a monk who'll be unable to to identify the figure—just some local saint, he'll say. So much for keeping accurate tabs on miraculous women.) Part of the market is about shopping; part of it is about eating. I don't just mean the restaurant stalls serving patrons who align themselves along low benches. I mean the vendors hanging big slabs of fatty meat from hooks beside hamhocks and tripe, the baskets of greens stacked beside baskets of spices and herbs and fruit. I mean the woman who's accosting me now, shaking a chicken by its plucked neck, not far from cages of live, still-feathered hens. Along the edges of the market, men selling alum stand behind big sacks of their product, a white substance chopped into blocks. The periphery of the market dwindles off into random vegetable stands, sellers of postcards and flowers. At the final corner, I pass an apothecary's shop with a monkey who may later be turned into a remedy for some ill. If I were an enterprising local, I'd print t-shirts for tourists with the slogan "I survived the market in Hue." Survived the heat, the maze of narrow passages, the noise, the hands grabbing me, the voices demanding "take this, buy this, give me money, give me your hat," the children shouting "yo, yo, yo" like an inner-city gang greeting a bunch of home boys.

I have to admit I've enjoyed the experience, the bustling body contact, the grins, the ferocious bargaining, the toothless old women, and the elegant old man lounging in his hammock strung in front of his stall. I cross over the curved stone bridge on the road behind the market and watch the wooden sampan boats lined up to unload their wares. Yes, the water's vile below me, full of garbage, a couple of men pissing into the sluggish current. Yes, it's terrible to think of the homes and houseboats downstream where women will dip their buckets in this river, soap their laundry. But, I suppose that if you don't think too hard about it, water retains its cleansing properties. It's the same water that's been here on earth ever since the planet began. We've polluted it over and over. Environmentalism means trying to clean that water up. Maybe faith means forgetting where the water's been before it reached your lips. Or maybe that's just the lie we tell ourselves, the intentional ignorance we call survival.

August 18, Hue

Lana and I are sitting in an open-air, circular thatched-roof restaurant that resembles an enormous tiki hut. It rises on pillars out of a large swamp that lies near one of the ornate stone gates that once defined the imperial city of the emperors. To reach the restaurant, we have crossed a sort of bridge over the swamp, an ambiance that we imagine must breed malaria-infested mosquitoes, a place that we would more cordially, more environmentally consciously call a wetlands, except that we are sure that the toilet hole in the rustic bathroom empties directly into the soggy grounds below.

It's time for lunch but we're the only clients. Everyone else in the place seems to be part of the staff or part of the family or maybe both. Clearly, portions of the restaurant double as a home. The males are asleep on cots that lie partially behind some patterned screens. The females are in that dubious state of half-on-duty and half-not, watching some melodrama on the television. Some of them sit on straight chairs facing the t.v. screen, some of them recline across a row of chair seats; all of them are completely absorbed in the emotional throes of the actress on the t.v., tossing hysterically in her hospital bed between bouts of traumatic flashbacks from her past. Hero-ically, one young woman tears herself away from the drama and de-scends upon us with menus. Lana begins to quiz her about the available kinds and sizes of bottled water. The normal fare in Vietnam is an unassuming mineral water housed in very large or very small plastic containers with a seal around the top that bears instructions in En-glish cautioning the buyer to reject the product if the seal's been broken. (Unscrupulous sellers have been known to fill recycled bottles with the ordinary stuff from the tap, a drink engendering dysentery or at least diarrhea.) When we're lucky, the water's cold. But today, Lana's thirsting for a liquid in a highly specialized version; she's requesting a certain medium-sized glass bottle of water that's fizzy but not sweetened. I don't think the waitress understands either Lana's gestures or her English, but she agrees to everything, and eventually a younger girl comes by the table with a bottle in a bucket of ice, something she's clearly gone down the street to fetch. But it's not what Lana had in mind; she waves it away. I feel guilty for the trouble the girl has gone to; I don't want her to classify us under the stereotype of demanding tourists. I suggest a bottle of ordinary water, like ordering the "house wine" in a bar.

With the issue of beverages happily resolved, we concentrate on food; we read the menus and find them so entertaining we don't mind that it takes a while for the waitress to detach herself again from the melodrama on the t.v. Some of the entertainment arises simply from faulty spellings in English, turning the ordinary into exotic fare, such as "prepaped fish sauce," "fried pomato," and "pork pieces scrued with boiled vermicell." But some of the other entries strike us as mysterious, even poetic: "fried rice with meat of heart and ridned," "haft cooked beef mixed up lemon juice" and "soared a lot of slices of beef in vinegar." Some are cryptic: "rice and chopped" or "a meal white rice and foods." Others tell us more than we'd want to know: "some vegetables foods with onion, tomato, garlic, scallion, bean etc." or "boiled chicken shaken in pieces with salt and pepper." Then there are offerings that seem simply redundant: "cocacola—coke" or "fried shrimp wrapped sauted shrimp." Sometimes, reading the French version printed between the English and the Vietnamese helps us decipher the menu. Sometimes it doesn't. Nothing can explain the difference between "fried eel without water" and "roasted eel-fish without water." At least these are clearly different from "boiled chicken with greases." Our favorite listing resides in the duck category, just below the entry for "cooked duck with juice." It says "boiled dick with sauce of fish and gingeng." We are sure that this would cook any macho male's juice.

By the time the waitress returns, we're ready to place our less-than-adventurous orders for pho bo, a rice noodle soup with beef that when it arrives I swear tastes vaguely like dish water. It's the cilantro, says Lana, spooning up her broth with more gusto than I can manage. The soup doesn't matter really. What I have a taste for is the language of the menu. I want to take my copy in its plasticized enclosure home. And luckily, that's a matter more easily arranged than finding the right sort of bottled water. "Toi muon," I say, "I want," pointing to the menu, pantomiming the placement of it inside my purse. Okay, why not, the waitress shrugs, happy to let me pocket it, relieved to get back to the fan turning in the humid heat and the sweaty passions of the soap opera pouring from the screen.

August 18, Roaming the Outskirts of Hue

After lunch, we cross a small bridge to a district that seems heavily influenced by the Chinese but with a playfully Vietnamese spin on the look of its many pagodas, meeting halls, and temples. On one set of stairs, concrete dragons serve as banisters, painted in bright primary reds, blues, and yellows, with red balls topping the wires that spiral antenna-fashion from their heads. Another courtyard features odd beasts that seem part lion, part dragon, part horse. To their left, one wing of a low wooden-roofed building houses a barber shop with a drawn blue curtain serving as its front wall; the wing to the right holds a beauty parlor with rows of nail polish on a ledge and one of those old-fashioned helmet-style hair dryers on a pedestal behind a plastic armchair. In the middle, the temple itself backs up this melange of beasts and beauty. Down the street, a smaller temple seems to be aimed at children; in its yard stand painted pairs of wooden elephants, horses, and cranes whose backs beckon toddler-sized worshippers to take a ride. The animals surround a tiny red and gold throne stationed beneath a miniature pagoda. The scene reminds me of the playgrounds outside MacDonalds restaurants, a place for aspiring emperors of burgers to practice holding court. At intervals along the street, women vendors coalesce into a market, squatting over their baskets, their red and blue plastic tubs of grain and vegetables and dried fish; they make a sea of bobbing conical woven hats, headgear that seems paradoxically sturdy and as delicate as rice paper. Dong Ba, the central giant market, is the mall; these are the corner groceries.

When I stop to chat in English with one of the vendors, a crowd of women gathers around us—their matching baggy cotton pants and blouses making an explosion of color, of stripes and plaids and flowered prints. The vendor can't believe that both she and I are forty-eight. It's true that even though she's maybe not so wrinkled as I am, she does look older; life hasn't been as hard on me, and partly the difference is just a trick of fashion; she wouldn't be caught dead in the youthful shorts and tennis shoes and funky sunhat that I'm wearing. Although shop windows are filled with American fifties style ruffled blouses and short-sleeved polka dot shirtwaist dresses, I've never seen anybody actually wearing them. I suspect they also don't get married in the equally fifties-style prom growns featured in bridal shops. I'd bet they spend most of their lives in the shirts and pants they're all wearing now, while they surround me, pointing to my sunhat whose broad brim is composed of cloth stretched on bamboo struts, a contraption that can be folded up accordion-style into the size of a closed fan and tucked neatly into a purse or travel bag. I've learned that this hat is a guaranteed conversation piece, especially in a country accustomed to more stubbornly uncollapsible headgear woven from reeds. Now, I take off the hat and fold it, a ruse to draw the women's attention away from my camera while I pretend to take a photo of the vendor and her daughter. Really I'm focusing on an elegantly tough old woman who's got a two-handed grip on her lighter, lifting it to a cigarette the size of a Cuban cigar. My subterfuge doesn't work, but the old woman doesn't seem to mind that I've snapped her photo; she waves her cigarette, amused. Down the block, I find Lana kneeling over a pile of second-hand clothes spread on a sheet on the ground, digging through them like an avid shopper at a garage sale. Another female flock has surrounded her, intrigued that a foreigner would show such interest in such ordinary merchandise. One of the women has artificial legs and feet so doll-like that the limbs of mannikins seem more realistic. I don't want to think about the bombs or post-war land mines that might have crippled her, don't want to be sidetracked away from this moment of animatedly joyful sisterhood into the memory of the evils that have divided us. I focus instead on a woman with salt and pepper hair, her legs planted stoutly apart, her shirt straining to button over her equally stout stomach. Her teeth have been blackened to fulfill an earlier ideal of beauty. I lift my camera, trying to attune the press of the shutter to the rhythm of her smiles. It will be weeks before the film's developed, before I know whether I've caught that charcoaled grin.

We keep wandering, detouring from the streets to the frequent paths leading to the river where girls in their pajama cottons topped by ribboned straw hats wash clothes. Clearly, foreigners are rare in this part of town. How do I know? A. There is no bottled water for sale. B. No cyclo drivers pass, looking for a fare. C. There are no motorbikes. The world is exceptionally quiet. D. People seem astounded by our presence, interested in us, their children following us only to look and listen, not to yell or ask for something. Instead, they seem thrilled just to wave and say hello. It's a delightful part of town, residential and tree-lined, leafy with shade in the heat, with some downright prosperous homes boasting neoclassic columns and festooned with balconies. Many of them seem old but well maintained, the starkness of their painted concrete walls softened by curves and touches of pillars and porches, each home accompanied by a bit of yard and trees and bushes, often with shrines and potted plants. Mixed in are bits of ruins of the gates of the earlier, imperial city, and more modest wooden houses, plus the latest concrete suburban two-storey kitsch with bottom floors resembling a garage or breezeway, the overall effect as tasteless as suburbia is in any country.

We take a road that cuts through fields past a cemetery, a route fronted by much smaller dwellings with their wooden or corrugated tin roofs lined up shoulder to shoulder along the dust that functions as a yard and a street. There's laundry strung between the porch poles, one place with a row of posts like connected toothpicks, each one topped by a pair of wet cotton underwear. We run into a man who's strapped a radio and cassette player inside a large box mounted over his bike's back wheel, along with two boxes for speakers and, wired just behind the handlebars, a car battery to power his mobile music. He's a kind of traveling disc jockey, making a mockery of the stores back home that claim to sell "car toys." He's rightfully proud to pose for a photo documenting his technological achievements.

A girl on a red bike, wearing a cross between an army hat and a big-visored baseball cap, begins to ride silently beside us. We communicate by periodically grinning. After she's accompanied us for about a mile through the flat fields, I suddenly jump onto the bike's back fender, and she amazes me with her strength, peddling steadily forward till we both collapse with laughter. Another mile down the road, we near a settlement of houses and she motions for me to straddle the fender again. I oblige and we pass into what must be her neighborhood because other kids and adults in the yards shout and wave to her, while she giggles so hard I'm afraid we'll crash into the ditch. But hey, if peddling a middle-aged foreigner through her local turf increases her status, then I'm willing to hang on. Beyond the houses, a crane labeled U.S. Army (what must be left-over or appropriated goods) is working on a bridge. I want to document this shift in power but I don't want any zealous Vietnamese guard to arrest me for snapping pictures of domestic infrastructure improvements being carried out by former imperialist military hardware. I position the girl and her bike in front of the crane; they'll serve as my alibi. "Why, officer, I was only taking a photo of your impressive young countrywoman. You must be so proud of her— such a friendly girl, so beautiful and so strong."

Since the bridge is under construction, impassable for either pedestrians or cylists, Lana and I give the girl a farewell handshake and board a long narrow boat with an upswung bow to cross the canal. The boat is powered by a woman wielding a long pole. I'll never really understand the action of these boats; the pole seems to swivel within the confines of a rag or rope, the poler not pulling back against the water in the action I'd call rowing, only turning the pole like a scythe through grain, but somehow the boat moves forward. On the far shore, red-roofed houses rise above wooden stilts on concrete pillars driven into the water's edge. On our ferry, one of the passengers is a little girl who's operating as the local version of pizza deliverer, only her take-out load is a bowl of tiny steamed crabs, plus a small dish of salt and other seasonings. She hands a crab to the woman poling the boat. Maybe it's a tip? I'm never entirely sure how to interpret what happens here. My uncertainty mirrors the general traveling situation where a sign-up sheet appears at some tourist cafe but whether there'll be enough names to fill a bus and whether a bus will be available remains a mystery until the designated hour when the driver is or isn't honking at the hotel door.

August 18, Dinner at the Grand Hotel

I'm a dedicated budget traveler. This stance is partially political, partially dictated by the size of my income. Sometimes when I've splurged on a more expensive vacation, I've found myself regretting it, overcome with longing for what I consider the real taste of a country—an atmosphere that lies elusively beyond the reach of luxury tourist junkets. Once, I spent a week at a posh resort that had unfortunately sprung up on what used to be my favorite beach outside Puerto Vallarta, Mexico, a playa I used to reach by standing by the road for an hour, then crowding into a delapidated mini-van known as a combi. One afternoon, lying back in the waves beside what had been transformed from deserted sands to a sprawling complex of buildings fronted by fake waterfalls spilling under concrete bridges, I heard the grind of a diesel-spewing bus fighting its way up the steep grade of the road that led past the hotel. A rush of nostalgia filled me; I wanted to board that bus again, take it wherever it led, knowing that the destination didn't matter. The bus itself was Mexico, overloaded and alive with the smells of sweat and chicken feathers and hand-ground tortillas.

Still, a part of me loves luxury, and I've always maintained that you can talk leftist politics while enjoying the amenities of a yuppie fern bar. Watching the path of the full moon and the lights of the city of Hue reflected in the ripples of the river passing just beneath this hotel terrace, I admit that I could happily engage in the comforts of much more up-scale travel.

Until tonight, Lana and I have always turned left outside our hotel's door, dodging the water vendors, heading toward the bridge that passes into the main town. This evening we turned right and discovered that only a few blocks from our converted horse stable lies a haven of luxury hotels and shops that cater to their clients. We've spent the pre-dinner hours trying on the silk suits and dresses in the shops, perusing the bolts of patterned cloth. We haven't exactly satisfied the clerks' hopes for big commissions, but we've done our proletarian best, picking up a couple of blouses and a few meters of fabric for a friend back home who's commissioned us to buy her some silk at less than State-side prices.

We suspect that if our faces weren't clearly foreign, we couldn't have walked so brazenly and unaccosted up the meticulously tended paths of this hotel in our shabby traveling clothes. Even now, after we've staked out our rights to this river-side table, the waiter is not sure we belong, takes his time about delivering our drinks. We've agreed that we'll just have a drink, check out the menu and, if the prices are manageable, we'll stay for dinner. Otherwise, it's back to the restaurant at the Marin. The prices turn out to be borderline, so we stay, seduced by the quiet, the pattern of lights on the water, the boats passing silently below us.

I don't want to believe in the power of money, but I want to believe that if you spend your hard-earned cash, you get your money's worth. We don't. The meal is mediocre. It's only the lights and the moon and the water that have really delivered. Walking home, we pass some local fishermen lounging on the river bank, taking in for free what we've just paid too much for.

August 19, the Perfume River

A boat is the only civilized way to travel here, free from the noise of motorbikes. Our boat is simple: an unadorned hull housing a wooden cabin the size of a small bedroom, the outer walls painted a faded blue and yellow emblazoned with the words "Service Tourist." The bow is ordinary, not curved up into the giant figurehead of a dragon, lion, rooster or hen like the bows of the other tourist crafts. Inside, there are four plastic chairs and walls covered with prints of Asian couples in Western bride and groom wear with a jet flying above them, posters featuring a passle of fruit or a chubby naked baby in a straw hat. The Vietnamese man who's arranged our river tour keeps constantly repeating the terms of the bargain. He's the stereotype of the stressed business executive. He introduces us to a woman in the usual cotton print pajamas who, unusually, is the captain. We nod to everything he says, waiting graciously for him to disembark. Then we work out our real itinerary with the captain.

By lucky chance, the entrepeneur has thrown together an amiable crew of tourists—two young Englishwomen, Lana, and me. We agree about all the sites we'd like to visit; we agree that the view from the Perfume River is reward enough: sandy banks backed by bush and trees, an almost jungle lushness punctuated by glimpses of sacred or imperial architecture and clusters of more modest homes, mountains in every hue of green and blue and purple, peaks lapping over themselves in the sun-drenched distance.

But this is supposed to be a tour, and so we disembark first at the Thien Mu Pagoda, a cylindrical beige stone tower composed of seven storeys, each smaller than the one below it like the layers of a wedding cake, each dedicated to a buddha who assumed a human form. According to legend, a fairy woman appeared to a governor of the province, instructing him to build a pagoda here. To me, what's impressive is not the pagoda, or the massive marble turtle symbolizing longevity, or the giant bell that could be heard ten kilometers away. It's the old pale blue Austin car parked behind the complex of religious buildings. In the sixties, this was a brewing ground for protest against the South Viet-namese government. A monk named Thich Quang Duc traveled to Saigon in this Austin to set himself afire in an act of protest against the Diem regime's crackdown on Buddhists. The front pages of newspa-pers around the world carried the photograph of Thich Quang Duc: a man sitting upright with his legs crossed, his body completely engulfed in flames—the only image that has ever made me see the buddha's lotus position as both sacrificial and calmly defiant. Just in case that scene hasn't already been burned into the mind of every visitor, some-one has placed a framed copy of the photo in the windshield of the Austin. In the face of that strength of will and dedication, I feel more than humbled, struck by the feebleness, even the vanity of my own gestures of protest. It's a shock to my sense of history as well. I realize I've always associated this and subsequent photos of immolated monks with protests against the U.S. and its role in the war—an ethnocentric spin my memory put upon such actions. Now I see my country as doubly indicted: napalming the Vietnamese in support of a ruler whose corrupt practices had led monks to "napalm" themselves. Not every visitor seems daunted by the monk's message. A bevy of professional photographers hovers around the site, laden with their camera gear, one of them positioning two young Vietnamese women in front of spots of interest. If I had the patience of a monk, I would shrug, say life goes on, even photographers have to earn a living somehow. Because I'm not a monk, I feel disgusted, turn away from the busy camera shutters, down the steps to our waiting boat.

Back on the river, I'm a tourist again, with a tourist's itinerary to fulfill. We stop next at the road leading to Tu Duc's tomb. Our guide book says that this emperor had fifty chefs who prepared fifty dishes served by fifty servants, and his tea was made from drops of dew. Despite his hundred and four wives, plus concubines, he had no chil-dren. The guide book doesn't mention how he felt about this, doesn't say whether he blamed his women or beat them for his own shortcom-ings. It does say that he admitted the mistakes he'd made in ruling and gave his tomb a name that means "modest." Along the hot and dusty road to the tomb, children and women mob us, pressing their wares of cold drinks against our skin, repeating the English phrases they've learned from previous foreigners: "Later," "no money now." They stick out their hands to shake and seal a bargain, knowing that we'll buy on the thirsty way back.

We pass fresh cow shit everywhere, but there's not an animal in sight—only the dirt path ringed by dry bushes with here and there a fat bamboo pedestal topped by a wooden box housing a shrine. Once, we strike off into a field that seems to be a short-cut, but then another tourist worries outloud about the possibility of land mines left over from the war—and I'm suffused with terror, watching every step, eager to get back to the theoretically safe main route.

At last, we turn off into a path into the forested grounds—a retreat that is hardly what I'd term modest. There's a pavilion for reciting poems beside a man-made lake replete with lotus blossoms, a run of moats and walls and towers. In a lovely setting of pine woods and lantana flowers, stand stone statues of Mandarin style warriors, elephants and horses. But so much of this is in disrepair, the colors worn away, the tiled roofs broken and faded, the murals and dragons fashioned of bits of blue and white china now chipped and worn. And still so much remains of previous grandeur—this is how Beijing's Forbidden City might appear, if it had fallen onto harder days. Among the buildings that occupy the site, one sign says "storehouse for royal paraphernalia," but the place is empty; in the room beside it, the so-called riff-raff have moved in—thin, sweaty men eating and intent on a hot game of cards.

After this scorching hike to Tu Duc's tomb, our group of tourists confers. We agree that we've sufficiently sampled the royal sights, but none of us is ready to cut short the peace of traveling down the river. We make a plan. We'll tell our captain we want to visit the tomb at the end of the line. We have no intention of actually undertaking the hike to this site; we'll disembark and hide somewhere beneath the trees until the requisite amount of time has passed. But when we disembark, the captain's smallest daughter accompanies us—a solemn girl that we've discovered can break into smiles when coaxed. We think the jig's up; the daughter will report our scam, will tattle to her mother when she finds that we weren't really serious about visiting this last tomb and have talked the family into motoring all this way for nothing. To save face, we walk to the tomb's gate. Luckily, it's a short, shaded walk, but we worry all the way about what the daughter will do if we don't undertake the royal tour.

It turns out that we've been paranoid. She doesn't bat an eye when we stop at the tomb's gate, refusing to pay the entry fee to visit what we think we've already seen enough of. Feeling ridiculously relieved, we buy a bunch of small fat bananas, hand one to the daughter, distribute the rest to children haunting the path to the boat.

The river seems more heavenly than the resting places of emperors hoping to ascend to heaven. The river itself is heaven, a peaceful run of gentle waves carrying enough exotic sights to save it from monotony. Sampans pass us with their heaped loads of sand or a stack of logs—conveyances so much more gracious, so much less macho than the logging trucks that barrel dangerously down the foggy tight-curved roads of my own Washington State. The sampans constitute more than vehicles, more than the tools of a job. They're home to families, mothers calling to their naked children playing in the shallows by the river shore, women stringing laundry beneath the boats' central bamboo canopies that are sometimes topped incongruously by t.v. antennas.

On the banks to our left stand the towers of imperial architecture. Behind lie the layers of green and burnt sienna hills rising into mountains. In the middle of the river, there's suddenly the finger of a peninsula, a flat plain like a savannah in sub-Saharan Africa with water buffaloes and cows grazing instead of elephants and gazelles.

Too soon, we're pulling up to our dock; the children on board are clamoring for souvenirs. They refuse my fistful of U.S. pennies—not good enough. But Lana's brought a supply of cheap Bic pens. The captain's tiny son draws pictures on his arms and face. A boy without the money to buy paper.

August 19, Facing the Mirror

I'm standing nearly motionless in the bathroom, braving the cloud of mosquitoes, concentrating on a two-step diagnostic task. Pressing my face close to the mirror so that I can see without my glasses, I turn back the upper and lower lids of my right eye: still red, but no longer a swollen rosy purple. A fleck of matter crosses the eye, and I count the seconds until another passes. Over a minute between flecks, and they are simply flecks, not gelatinous masses filming over my vision. I'm truly on the mend.

Having assessed my eye's health, I check out my psychic well being. I step back from the mirror and put on my new Vietnamese glasses. Lana's assured me that I look fine in them, but that's a friend's duty, to tell the little white lies we need when we're depressed. It's true that my friend Cynthia and I have made a pact that should one of us go blind, the other will truthfully assess our appearance and help correct it, substituting a different scarf for the one whose color doesn't match, tissuing away smudged lipstick. But as long as I'm not blind, only myopic, it's my own judgment of my face in these glasses that I have to live with. And I guess I can. The years of technological advances—even in Vietnam—have made the lenses thinner than my old ones. In these small wire-rimmed frames, I resemble a cross between a prim schoolmarm and a Marxist intellectual. Not exactly flattering, and not a complete rendition of the self I normally present to the world, but at least these are recognizable pieces of that composite identity. I could say that I've even become accustomed to wearing glasses, but that would be a lie; I've only temporarily resigned myself to them. I'm determined to get up on my hundredth birthday and lean over the sink, inserting my latest contact lenses between my freshly scrubbed wrinkles.

August 19, Hue

Lana and I have been in Vietnam for two weeks, but we can count the good meals we've had on less than the fingers of one hand. To what should we attribute this culinary disappointment? We're not sure. We know we've happily devoured the cuisine in Vietnamese cafes in the States. During the year I spent in China, I agreed with the foreigners who swore the best spot for Chinese food was San Francisco—not because of the skill of the chefs, but simply because the quality of available ingredients was better. In Shanghai, the only vegetable on the menu all winter was cabbage. But here in Vietnam, the markets over-flow with sumptuous produce and mounds of pungent spices in straw baskets. Maybe we're just too timid; we've been afraid to dine in the markets' tiny food stalls because the hygiene seems dubious, but at least the fare being offered in their pots looks and smells enticing. En-ticing is not a word we'd use for the choices on the menus that we've been handed in the restaurants which seem to repeat the same tired litany of dishes, all of them overly fried. Surveying the more interesting looking platters on the tables of the Vietnamese diners, we suspect that the restaurants provide two menus: one naming delicious dishes for the locals; the other listing some boringly unadventurous selections printed in English, the all-purpose language describing the one-size-fits-all ap-proach to foreign palates.

But we have high hopes for this dinner in Hue where our guidebook praises the city's specialities, particularly touting the food at a place run by a deaf proprietor. One of the special dishes is a rice noodle soup with marinated strips of beef, garnished by sprigs of herbal greens. The other is more complicated, involving the conjunction of a shrimp om-elette with a crepe. Broken into pieces in a bowl along with slices of star fruit and green banana, fresh leaves of herbs and a peanut sauce, it is rumored to be spectacular.

When we arrive at the address listed in the guidebook, something about the atmosphere doesn't feel right, so instead, we sit down at the place next door, taking over a rickety table at the edge of the street. A group of skinny children instantly surrounds us. I pull out my stack of postcards of Seattle, and within ten seconds, I'm apologizing to the late-comers. Sorry, the last postcard's gone, and no, I have no other gifts to grant you. A waitress who must be pushing ten years old hands us a menu whose specialities are named in red at the top; she points to the wall where an article about the restaurant that was published in *The New York Times* is taped, featuring the picture of a beautiful long-haired and lithe-limbed woman that the newspaper calls Miss Hue, a star associated with five-star cuisine in Vietnam. We look up from the article to find that same lovely woman wafting unselfconsciously be-tween the tables in a rosy-flowered silk dress, taking orders and deliv-ering. No one would suspect that she's an international celebrity.

After the first bite, we add this restaurant to our meager list of mouth-watering meals. We agree that its only drawback is the city's evening heat which is intensified by the warmth of the coals beneath the tiny skillets on the sidewalk stove that's tended by a woman in a loose sleeveless blouse of magenta and turquoise patterns. One hand spins the skillets on the fire, the other reaches constantly toward the table beside her for fistfuls of chicken, shrimp, or vegetables.

But why should the guidebook be so right about the tastes, and get the address of their origin wrong? We look around for the deaf propri-etor mentioned in the guidebook and notice that Miss Hue and the cook are communicating silently by signs that grow increasingly more des-perate when the fan cooling the cook breaks down. Still, not everyone converses by signs. We gave our order to a young girl who could clearly hear, and hear bilingually. She handles the English-speaking clients. An-other sister takes care of the foreigners who prefer French.

Half-way through the meal, the mystery resolves itself. The propri-etor sits down at our table. He's deaf but armed with a big poster he uses to explain his family to the hearing world. The poster features stick figures arranged in a genealogical fashion. Some can hear, some can't. There are x's drawn across the figures of the family mem-bers who have died. His gestures indicate that he loves every mem-ber of his family except for one also-deaf brother who just last year opened up a restaurant next door, in competition with this cafe that he's been running for nearly thirty years. He pantomimes two fists in combat. I wonder if he knows that the guidebook has undeservedly touted his brother's establishment instead of his own. I don't have time to ask. Both places are so packed that their tables spill illegally onto the sidewalk, blocking the public thoroughfare, and the police have just arrived to put an end to this kind of chaos. Miss Hue rushes up, with two fingers stuck between her lips in the sign of a whistle, and the proprietor scurries like his brother to grab tables, haul his diners back inside.

After we've all been jammed more legally between his walls, the owner busies himself with a maze of makeshift wires and outlets, readjusting the jerry-rigged electric wiring that feeds the refrigerator and the fans that churn above his clients to relieve the night's humidity. But really, our discomfort is nothing. The most important fan is the one that alleviates the heat of the coals that the cook continues to tend, her face and fingers signing her disgust with both temperatures and cops. She's a mistress of this sort of protest against police interference that probably happens every night. With the gestures of one hand, she registers her annoyance; with the other, she flips the succulent crepes that the guidebook should have accurately praised.

August 20, Hue

This morning, we tried to rent bikes at our hotel. I had a bike in China, a one-speed model, with the big round tires so stable that I could balance for some moments at a stop before I bothered to put my feet down on the pavement. At home, I ride my second-hand bike on tours around the lake or the neighborhood, attracting passersby who marvel at my resolute insistence not to participate in the acquisition of the latest gear. Instead of a rip-stop nylon bag, my bike sports a straw basket tied to the handlebars with shoelaces; as a helmet, I wear the sturdy woven reeds of my Chinese construction worker's hard hat.

But the rental bikes at the hotel seem untrustworthy. On every one I try, the front wheel or the handlebars become a scarily unmanageable mass of shudders. I'm not interested in braving the streets on such a shaky vehicle; I already consider the traffic chaos sufficiently intimidating. Lana keeps circling around the courtyard on her own set of wheels, waiting for me to make up my mind. Either she's lucked onto a better bike or it's just that's she's so much younger than I am, not burdened by middle-aged doubts about the stability of wheels and handlebars and knees. I can't (or won't) risk it, I tell her, and get my money back from the rental guys who don't even bother to try to hide their derisive snickers (I ought to charge them for the entertainment my unsuccessful attempts at riding have provided).

Lana and I agree to meet at a certain pavilion inside the old imperial city of Hue. In the past, we've had some disagreeable moments of misunderstanding occasioned by this system of splitting, then meeting up. That's the sort of hitch that happens when you're traveling. This morning, we synchronize our watches, trying to accommodate the disparity between the time it will take to cycle there and the time it will require on foot. But once I've turned off the main road onto a route built above a swampy stretch of green that reminds me of a moat, and passed through the deep arch cut in the now-blackened stone of the tall pagoda-style gate that leads into the grounds of the ancient capital, I realize we haven't allowed for the time required to absorb the sense of devastation. Admittedly, a few of the palace buildings here have been restored to some semblance of their former grandeur, with golden layers of newly tiled roof rising above redecorated columns, and the pedestrian boulevards below them freshly paved with stones. But once upon a time, these palace grounds were extensive; now they're mostly fields and rubble. A result of the war. I sit down in the dusty courtyard facing a formerly elegant gate with three arches and layers of carved eaves rising above them, the stones stained with ruin now like streaks of mascara on the weeping face of an old whore. A pair of fire-blackened doors hangs ajar, doors whose red-grained wood still shows the traces of enameled dragons, fish, and lions. I swear I can smell the smoke of the bombs and fires and hand-to-hand combat that destroyed this place. More than ever so far, I feel the impact of the war. But why should this particular destruction move me even more than the destruction I see on the bodies of the people? Is it because people seem to be a renewable resource (however heartless that idea seems in the abstract), and the art and architecture of this place seem a one-time thing, a feat of imagination that will never be produced again? And what does the destruction of the gracious, graceful buildings of this ancient portion of the city tell us about the usefulness of radar and the other tools of military intelligence? Why destroy this place? It wasn't a factory or some other sort of functioning military target. But it was a symbol of the country's history and culture. Maybe that was deemed more important to destroy than any makeshift structure housing the manufacture of enemy munitions. A people's morale is based in their long-standing monuments, in their arts, not their armament factories. The Pentagon understood that. So why, I wonder, are the members of my country's current Congress wiping out the budget of the National Endowment for the Arts, while giving the military billions more than its generals have requested? It's as if the members of Congress are flying in the face of their own war logic, bombing their own nation's morale.

I sit so long, staring at the doors, that I'm late making my way to our appointed meeting place. And even then, I only wave across the courtyard, signing to Lana that I'm off on my own. The sight and smell of those devastated doors has undermined my ability to be sociable; I need to confront the emotions of this place alone. Lana jumps back on her bike, heading into the paths between the grassy mounds that have sprung up over the remains of the old city. I turn left, following a foot-path, listening to the spiel of a French guide leading a group of her country's tourists, a woman ignoring her own nation's imperialist role in Vietnam, its complicity in the various examples of war damage that she's busy pointing out. The Americans this, the Americans that, she explains. But not this American I want to tell her. Instead, I hurry past the group into a darkened room with altars of red and gold wood placed before small stage sets with their red curtains drawn back to reveal miniature thrones holding containers topped by cloths. Maybe a kind of funerary chamber for the emperors. An eerie, surreal space.

Outside the building stand some royal funeral urns taller than my-self, brass kettle shapes supported on three legs like witches' caul-drons, their rounded sides covered with raised reliefs of animals, sea creatures, horse-drawn carriages, and canyons. Beyond them, at the edge of the courtyard, flowering trees are resurrecting themselves from the effects of bombs and napalm. Some things heal, almost seamlessly; some things disappear, buried under the grass that miraculously grows back. Eventually, the war won't be written on bodies: the maimed will die, and after them, the children marred by deformities stemming from the curse of military chemicals that have poisoned the water and the earth. I'm not a scientist; I don't specialize in estimating how many generations that will take. I'm a writer; I believe in art. I know that even if the population should survive into an unscathed time, those doors of the imperial city will still swing on their broken hinges, a scar that can't be erased.

1991, The Gulf War

The destruction of Hue reminds me of the way the U.S. media doesn't show the reality of war anymore. No more front page photos of monks setting themselves on fire, no t.v. scenes of napalmed children, no nightly count of the soldiers returning home in body bags. I think the Gulf War was the first one in which the media totally exchanged their role of information-provider for that of handmaiden to the government. Mercifully, I escaped most of that pseudo-coverage since I was teaching in Tunisia at the time. But my friends tell me the media presented the war as a video game, so-called smart bombs attacking abstract targets. I caught a gist of that spirit the night the carpet-bombing of Baghdad began. Searching through the static on my shortwave radio, I picked up the voice of UPI, announcing coverage of the Gulf War "event," as if it were the Indianapolis 500 race. And it was, indeed, like that race where so much of the guilty pleasure seems to stem from watching the car wrecks. Only the media weren't reporting the war's wrecks. No station aired footage of the U.S. tanks plowing across Iraqi trenches, burying the soldiers alive, a clear violation of the so-called chivalry of battle. Nor did they show the carnage after the U.S. bombed what turned out to be a shelter for Iraqi civilians. The day after that happened, I entered the teachers' lounge at the University of Tunis, and pointedly, nobody talked to me.

I do believe the protests shut down the U.S.-Vietnam war, but I also believe those protests were fueled not simply by the activists in the streets but the people at home confronting the visions on the nightly news. Every evening those napalmed bodies entered American living rooms, reminding us that "collateral damage" wears a human face. But these days, the latest Christmas toy is a bombed-out shell of a doll's house, billed as a command center from which your child can "realistically" direct the battle.

August 20, Back on the River

I admit that I've been keeping this journal basically optimistic. Today, I'll tell the whole truth. The reminders of the war depress me, as do the capitalistic signs of the latest assault by the forces of the West, led by the rules that the World Bank and the International Monetary Fund impose on so-called developing countries—rules that so often dictate belt-tightening for the poor, a Mercedes for the rich—rules that too often seem to undermine the indigenous fabric of the country, intent on turning the world into a homogenous string of skyscrapers and Big Macs—a vision that constitutes one of my ideas of hell.

But to tell the truth is not only to rail against the future that the latest version of imperialism has in mind. To tell the truth is to admit that the tentacles of materialism and greed have already taken hold, that even the present is not what I'd expected. This country's not so peaceful and gentle as my own imagination and my guide book have led me to suspect. I could happily strangle the inventors of the motorbike and horns. Every place is too dusty; sometimes it's too hot, even for a devotee of heat and sun like myself. In a city like Saigon, the rampant commercialism (or the willingness to succumb to it) disappoints me. That letdown reminds me of a trip I took during my year in China. All the foreign teachers had been seduced by the tales of Guilin, a city set beside the Li River whose banks were lined with the sort of cloud-encircled jagged peaks we'd seen painted over and over on Chinese scrolls. And so, of course, during our school vacation, we'd made our way to Guilin, only to find a drab concrete city filled with urchins asking for a hand-out and everybody else from taxi drivers to restaurant owners to hotel clerks demanding that we grease their palms with foreign hard currency rather than the local Chinese renminbi that we—like the rest of the country's workers—received as salaries. Guilin became symbolic of the depths of disappointment—a kind of standard by which to measure everything else. Afterwards, whenever a friend returned from a trip, we'd ask, "Was it as bad as Guilin?"

So far, nothing in Vietnam has been as much of a disappointment as Guilin. But because I've sworn to tell the truth today, I admit this second boat ride on the Perfume River feels as if it might turn out to rival Guilin. Except for the fact that I'd forgotten my camera, the day's excursion didn't begin badly. Life tends to feel and look good here, as long as you're on the river. Lana and I boarded in good spirits, linking up with Ziggy, a German actress we became friends with in Dalat and ran into again last night in Hue—the three of us ending up at the same "floating restaurant" on the river, sharing a fan that provided respite from the heat and mosquitoes.

As always, the river banks have been thick with green foliage, and lots of activity—people swimming, bathing, washing clothes and pots. As always, we've been impressed by the population's ability to believe in the illusion that water cleanses just because it's liquid—even though some guy is pissing next to where some girl is washing dishes. We've passed water buffaloes with only the head and horns visible above the surface of the stream. We've passed sampans with their light curved hulls flitting over the current like dragon flies, their fishing nets strung behind them like a mesh of wings. We've answered hello to kids shouting and waving on the shore; some of them have pantomimed the motions of shooting as we passed, but I haven't seen this as specifically hostile. I'd expect the same from children in the States—the result of watching too much prime-time t.v.

It's not the menacing gestures of a few children on the shore that depresses me. It's the male children pretending to be men in charge of our boat that has me worried. I suppose they could be as old as eighteen. I suppose this barrier of wooden pylons where we've been waiting along with a host of other boats for two hours could be termed a " canal lock." The rumor is that when the tide's right, the waters will rise high enough to rush over this barrier and ferry us onto the other side so our boat can reach the beach we've paid to spend the day on. Nobody we ask seems quite sure about when and whether this tidal action will happen. Meanwhile, our boat has become the party craft; ten guys from other boats have boarded to lie around smoking, playing tapes on the cassette deck. I wonder just how that machine is powered. I haven't seen either batteries or a source of electricity on board.

Ziggy and I lie back in the sun, trying to concentrate on the books we've hauled along. Lana, however, has reached the end of her stock of patience, and besides that, she needs a bathroom. I watch her approach the edge of desperation and decide I have to do something about this. "Take us back," I tell the greasy teenager in charge of our boat, and a shouting match ensues. We've already paid his employer for most of our fare; if we return now, he's afraid we won't pay the balance, and he'll get nothing. I'm not concerned about this sort of economics. I'm concerned about my traveling companion's mental state. "We want to go back," I shout. "No," he yells. "Yes," I say, determined that I can say yes more times than he can say no. And so we continue this one-word exchange for longer than I care to imagine. Eventually, our young captain resorts to body language to engage my sympathies. He wrinkles up his face, tears his hair in clearly faked little boy gestures, squeezing out some little boy crocodile tears. "Excuse me, excuse me," he whines. "I don't understand." But I can tell he understands perfectly, and I refuse to fall victim to this "mama's boy" act. Only minutes before, I watched him constantly pulling out his pocket mirror to check his pompadour hair style, to peruse his face for pimples, then lean back, admiring his reflection. Maybe this kind of whining victim act worked with his mother, but it's not going to work with me. Suddenly, after all this waiting, the water rushes over the pylons, and the assembled boats become a melee of passing the barrier, banging into each other, threatening to rip off the bamboo poles that serve as oars and the arms that row them.

Saved by the tide, our whiney captain gets busy chasing the freeloaders off our boat, trying to station our craft so that we won't be capsized. Lana confides that she's okay now, and I feel like I've put myself on the line for nothing. My blood pressure tells me that I should travel only in countries where the prices, the itineraries, and the tides are clearly set—or at least I should pay the extra money for an organized tour from some hotel, not put myself at the mercy of greasy, grinning, sleazily stubborn guys. Nostalgically, I remember how easy the world seemed only a day or so ago, on that boat trip captained by a woman.

Finally, we reach the town beside the water's other shore. The youngest boy from the boat insists on accompanying us to the beach. Probably, he's been sent along to make sure we'll return and pay the balance of our fare. We think we should take him hostage to be certain that the boat will be there when we're ready to return.

But the beach itself is lovely—long, mostly deserted stretches of sand, with equally deserted stretches of awnings and beach chairs meant to be rented to tourists. Since we constitute one of the few tourist groups, we're paid more than our share of attention by the vendors. Little girls come by, intent on selling peanuts. We try a handful. Later, they return, trying to approximate how many we've consumed. We pay over and over for the same bunch of bananas. We can't fault the vendors for such errors in their accounting. We're tourists, and all tourists look alike.

The little boy who's accompanied us is beckoning. Time to relinquish the sands and the waves. Time to follow him back through the narrow streets of town to catch the lift of tides that will waft us over the barrier of poles that divides the river. On the long passage to the dock near our hotel, I keep a watchful eye on the teenaged captain in his greasy pompadour, aware that for him, I represent the depths of frustration and disappointment, a symbol like Guilin. The feeling's mutual then, I think, and know that this time I've told the whole truth.

August 21, The End of Hue

We've checked out of our room, but it will be several hours before the bus arrives to take us to Hanoi, so we've stacked our bags behind the reception counter, beside mounds of other tourists' luggage and back packs. (Later, we'll find that this was not a smart move; our bags will be crawling with ants occasioned by the bread and fruit stashed in one of the back packs.)

Time to kill means we head up the street and turn aimlessly at a new corner, some place to get lost in till we have to find our way back. The maze of streets deposits us outside a temple mobbed by worshippers celebrating something. A line of young monks passes, affecting punk defiance in their hair styles: shaved heads but sporting one long swatch of hair in front. We squeeze between the crowds of people lined up for bowls of feast day food, pass the funerary photos of the dead, and find ourselves in front of a courtyard altar, where the faithful in long grey tunics kneel to address the candles and flowers positioned between columns painted with the characters of the Vietnamese language, each pillar a vertical run of messages. We hang back at the entrance to the altar, feeling daunted by the solemnity of the worshippers. But the children seem unaffected by either the ritual or the need to be quietly hesitant in the face of it. They gather around us to recite their set of memorized questions in English: "Where you from? What your name? How old you are? What do you want to do? Where go? How long you stay in Vietnam?" They don't listen to the answers, which probably don't fit whatever model they've been taught in school. Instead, they keep asking until they've exhausted their stock of questions; then they simply start their list again from the top. In a way, they remind me of my own students back home, students who are native speakers, born and raised in English as their mother tongue, but mostly not listening, asking me to explain for the twentieth time just what I mean by next week's assignment. I'm on vacation now, and not obligated to repeat myself over and over. I nudge Lana away from the temple, disentangling myself from the children's rote recitation of questions, and we fade into the street, a good getaway down an alley that opens into a small market where we fill our travel purses with bananas, dragon fruit, and peanuts, a cache of food that will fortify us on the miles to Hanoi.

August 21, On the Bus to Hanoi

We're excited because the bus is big and modern, with comfortable seats and air conditioning. Mostly, we're delighted because we've clearly passed the last pick-up spot for passengers in Hue and there are only seven of us now, leaving plenty of space to stretch out. Everyone will have two seats to recline across, an important factor given that the bus ride began at five p.m. and we're not scheduled to arrive in Hanoi before ten tomorrow morning. We plaster our eyes to the windows to take in the outskirts of Hue: the typical Vietnamese architectural mix of the faded grandeur of emperors and French colonizers, the modern prosperous stucco kitsch, and in between these, the concrete simplicity that—when it's aesthetically pleasing—signifies poverty, and signifies official buildings when it's just plain ugly.

Our euphoria about the spaciousness of the bus continues through sunset, which always seems to arrive here too early. I'm still accustomed to Seattle summer evenings where the northern bent of the sun provides light long into what would otherwise be called night. But we're in luck not just in terms of buses but also in terms of planets. There's a full moon rising as the sun gives up, and so the landscape continues to function under its eerie glow.

Not everything functions as well as the moonlight. The roads are the first thing to break down as we head past the DMZ (the so-called Demilitarized Zone where some of the heaviest military action occurred in the U.S.-Vietnam war and where at least 5,000 locals have since been injured or killed by the left-over mines and military firepower). As we enter what was once the separate state of North Vietnam, the roads resemble the greater Chicago metropolitan area in summer—a morass of continuous construction, unpeopled by workers. And unmarked as well: no stock of flares or rows of plastic orange and white-striped barrels to indicate the paths we should take. Instead there are sudden mounds of chunky gravel, one-lane detours around heaps of rock. If we're lucky, they're marked by the empty barrels that the tar arrived in. Mostly, we're not lucky. But I don't resent this construction the way

I often do in the States where the existing highways seem acceptable enough and the logic of tearing them up eludes me. This is the main road north to Hanoi and its condition has clearly been unacceptable for a long time. The road is one evil series of bumps and potholes, the remains of an infrastructure destroyed by the U.S. government and its bombs during the war that I remember as both the backdrop and the focus of my college and early graduate school years, as the higher education of campus protests and the birth of my own political consciousness.

Even at a crawl, the bus jolts and lurches. I owe my Uncle Sam the credit for this jarring ache climbing up my spine. I try to concentrate on the moon-lit view, to place my attention outside my temporary pain and the much greater pain that attended the massacre of these roads—the mix of hubris and tragedy that we call a war. The bus weathers the jolts, but the driver begins to break down, announcing in French that he's ill with a cold or the flu. We'll pull off, he says, and stop, maybe at some hotel. But this is not what we've bargained for. We've agreed to a seventeen-hour journey; we've had no idea that the bus company would expect the same man to chauffeur the whole trip, especially not a man suffering from the flu. Selfishly, we urge the driver on. The landscape outside the window becomes a moonscape of white sand or salt; the road climbs, rounding some cliffs, with a darkness that must be the sea in the forefront. I worry about the driver's state of control, picture a flu-inspired fever plunging us over the edge.

Around 10 p.m., the driver makes the first of several attempts at long-term stops. He pulls off beside a hotel in a town where all the women seem to wear black and white polka-dotted blouses. We refuse the hotel, compromise on a stop for dinner or naps at the local family-run restaurant. There's no menu and no discussion concerning what we might wish to eat or what the restaurant offers. Instead, the polka-dotted women simply arrive at our tables with the Vietnamese idea of foreigner fare: tired baguettes and a processed cheese spread wrapped in triangles of foil that bear a picture of some black and white Holstein under a brand name in French that translates as the laughing cow. I've spread this same smiling cow across my breakfast bread for several days now. It's an edible cow, but not exciting enough to entice me when I'm not truly hungry.

I am, however, truly longing for a bathroom. The driver has pulled over once for a pit-stop, but it was a male pit-stop where you open your pants-fly beside the road. Even in the semi-darkness of shadows, I wasn't prepared to drop my own pants and squat. I corner one of the polka-dotted women, and she gestures toward the back of the restaurant. I make my way through family rooms, then a precarious pitch down a narrow plank in the dark to a kind of outdoor deck. Next to a girl washing a plucked chicken in a basin, there's a square box like a free-standing closet set beside a pen of pigs. In the box, there's a hole to aim for.

The trip to the bathroom cheers me up. It reminds me of the year I lived in China and the deep nostalgia I still harbor for that country. It reminds me that I've dealt with major inconveniences before, that I've boarded buses crowded with sweaty human flesh and unplucked chickens, that I've squatted over plenty of squalid holes—and I can still do it. I'm ready to laugh good-naturedly at anything now, including the sleepless night of potholes that we're clearly up against, and the ants that accompany the platter of baguettes like an extra bit of protein.

After the driver has rested over his bowl of noodles and the tourists have argued with the owner over just how many of the baguettes and triangles of cheese spread they've actually consumed and should pay for, we drive on. We pass simple homes of mud and thatch or wood, lit with one candle or a kerosene lamp, isolate bits of flickering glow that engender small oases of warmth and light in the dark like a village of fireflies. The night acquires a surreal quality as groups of people suddenly and inexplicably materialize inside it, illuminated by our bus's headlights. They've gathered beside the road to sit or stand; sometimes they've assembled in the dead-center of the highway. At first I try to rationalize their presence, think they must be waiting for a bus. But a bus to where? And at this time of night? I remember the month I spent living on an island in Washington State in a cabin without electricity, remember the impossibility of doing much of anything by the light of candles or kerosene lamps. Every night, I gave up on attempts at reading, spent the hours until bed drinking in the bar just down the road. Here, in this countryside, the sparse gatherings of homes make their own islands, and the road itself becomes a kind of clubhouse, a place to socialize, to pass the darkness till your bones agree to rest.

Rest is what the bus driver is after. He stops again at a dimly lit hotel, but it must be closed or full or unwilling to cooperate with whatever terms he's offered. He comes back to the bus without comment, and starts the engine. The Frenchman in the front seat offers to spell him for two hours but the driver refuses out of a sense of pride or fear of retribution from his boss or maybe it's just plain illegal for a tourist to pilot other tourists.

We're all beginning to regret the bus's air conditioning. The night is now cool enough to do without the blast of artificial air that inspires our random fits of coughing. I'd like to curl up inside the one long-sleeved heavy cotton shirt that I've lugged unworn through Vietnam's hot and muggy August, but I know my bag is buried on the bottom of the pile of luggage. I wrap myself inside my bare arms instead, and stretch out on my sumptuous ration of two seats. Past midnight, we pull into a hub of activity: a line of over-loaded ancient trucks and local long-distance buses that, unlike ours, sag under the weight of bicycles and freight stacked on the roof and too many passengers stacked inside. The line is flanked by small stalls vending food and drinks, making a roadside respite of dim lanterns and feverish anticipation. Everyone's waiting for the ferry to cross the river. The driver descends and disappears into the realm of negotiations. Whatever rank he's pulled turns out to have been successful; we advance to the head of the line. And here's the ferry arriving, bogged down with traffic from the other side. The ferry is really a large metal raft, nudged·across the river by a small tugboat that's lashed to its side. The raft drops an open-work steel ramp to unload and load. Everything about this ferry seems makeshift and temporary. Before the years of bombs, there was probably a bridge here.

For some reason, most (but not all) of the passengers have to disembark and stand beside their vehicles during the trip across the river's brown waves. The combination of mysteriously arbitrary rules and jerry-rigged modes of transportation simply increases my nostalgia for China. Once upon a time, I took a ferry just like this one across China's Yangtse River. (Though I admit I was more star-struck then by the name of the river and all the associations it carried with it. And the ferry there was not occasioned by a lack of bridges due to bombs.) Tonight, I volunteer to get off the bus, to stand on the bits of metal raft beside it, in the darkness relieved by the full moon. I'm indulging in my own version of glorified romanticism, making myself part of some purposeful sense of mass movement: China's Long March to revolution or the Ho Chi Minh trail, some army of dedicated bodies surging forward on the tides of visions larger than their individual souls. Beside me, the engines grind, spewing diesel fumes. I transform that dirty cacophony into the strains of the "Internationale" or "The East Is Red."

I know that the victory of Mao's Long March was the best thing that could have happened to China then, freeing the country from the centuries of dominance by emperors and war lords and the years of dominance by foreign hierarchies when in Shanghai alone a hundred frozen penniless corpses could be retrieved each morning from the gutters. And—at least in theory—Mao's victory was a chance for women to hold up only half the sky (and get acknowledged for that) instead of holding up more than their share without an ounce of recognition, and doing that on bound broken feet. I also know that, later, the Chinese Cultural Revolution was a disaster, followed by the evils of the bloody assault on citizens trying to protect the ideals of the students occupying Tiannamen Square. I know that Vietnamese re-education camps were really prisons. So how can I stand on this ferry's metal deck and persist in this dream of collective positive endeavor? Maybe I just don't have enough ritual in my daily life. Or maybe just not enough opportunities for rituals that seem communally optimistic. My traveling companion Lana loves the country's temples with their hanging spirals of sweetly burning incense. My temple is a precarious raft trying out the possibilities of visions bigger than these silt-brown waves, the waters we try to negotiate under the dark of midnights lit by full moons.

August 22, Still on the Bus to Hanoi

Not everything about river crossings is romantic. The ramp didn't quite reach the shore and I sloshed through the last bits of river, glad I'd worn my rubber thongs, sorry I hadn't rolled up my pants. They stayed damp through the rest of the night, increasing the chill of the air conditioning on the bus while I drifted in and out of sleep, only half-consciously noting that the jolting motion of the road stopped for three hours while the driver napped.

It's dawn now, and we're on the road again, passing homes of white painted concrete with red-tiled roofs descending in a sloping curve, the oldest roofs turned the color of an aged corncob. The scene is more austere than the landscape of the south, but this austerity makes an elegance beside the green of foliage in the tiny yards and the fields. On the road, the population's headgear has also changed. I see more women wearing conical hats of woven reeds; the men have replaced the baseball caps of Saigon with green pith helmets. There are people with carts and ploughs drawn by Brahma cows and water buffaloes. There are bikes instead of motorbikes—although I do see one man ferrying his motorbike home on a cart pulled by a cow.

If prosperity equals Western kitsch and Western plastic, then there is less of that. But why complain about the so-called lack of progress when the tables and chairs and stools at a roadside cafe are made of a wood that matches the cafe's rustic walls, instead of being fashioned from some garish plastic? Even the mountains seem more rugged than their counterparts in the south, their sheer slabs of rock cutting through the vegetation's green. In the north, the brown dirt of the fields doesn't always nurture rice, and when it does, the fields are hemmed along their jigsaw puzzle edges with stands of corn. The greater ruggedness of landscape equals the greater ruggedness of life here—a ruggedness that I find appealing.

And then the north itself grows more lush and maybe even more lovely than the south, the mountains gathering themselves together into the jagged peaks that populate the inked landscape of ancient Chinese scrolls—but never quite that otherworldly and mysterious. It seems that every view in Vietnam includes either mountains or water: rivers, ponds, lakes, standing marshes, the wetness of the rice fields, and (visible or not) the sea that's never too far off. Just now, we're passing a marsh with a stand of pink lotus with blossoms bigger than the blowziest peonies. In the center of this blooming color stands a sign with words that must mean poison printed above the universal skull and crossbones that signifies deadly. But what could be deadly about the peaceful Buddha blossom of a lotus? Once again, the memory of the war tugs at the edges of my mind, ready to name itself responsible. Is this marsh polluted by military chemicals? By unexploded mines? Curiously enough, I have to admit that, outside the devastation of the imperial city in Hue and the stunted foliage around the tunnels at Cu Chi, I haven't seen that much evidence of the war's destruction in the architecture or the landscape. But maybe I just don't know what to look for. Or perhaps the evil is there but invisible to my untrained gaze—like the deadliness in these lotus flowers. In any case, I've been purposefully avoiding the war. Lana and I have agreed not to visit the DMZ or the military museums, sites where a downed plane or rusting tank takes the place of the bronze statuary that nations usually erect to commemorate some conflict. I don't really need the landscape to prompt my memories. I've read the signs of war on the limbless bodies of survivors and deformed children born after the plagues of Agent Orange. I've heard the violations recounted in the women's stories.

A train passes. We traverse the ugliness of suburbs. We enter a stretch of tree-lined boulevards and lakes, old French mansions, some kept up, some not. It's long past our original goal of ten a.m. But we're finally in Hanoi.

When I return to Seattle, a friend who's a Vietnam vet will ask me, "Where did you go on your trip?"

"All the way from Saigon to Hanoi."

"Yeah," he'll smile, "we tried that too."

August 22, Hanoi

It's one thing to manage to arrive in a city; it's something else to find a place to sleep there. The bus deposits us in a narrow side street busy with tiny shops and equally tiny restaurants specializing in the soup known as pho bo. Open on one side to the street, the restaurants feature two or three low tables and a stove surrounded by the soup's ingredients: boiled chickens, greens, spices, and noodles. There's only one hotel, whose tacky modern glass and steel facade appears incongruous in these surroundings. Inside, the price named by the two young women at the reception desk strikes us as too high. We take a cyclo to another hotel; it costs even more. Lana elects to accompany the cyclo driver to a place run by his brother which he swears we can afford. I wait with our luggage in the hotel's elegant lobby, slouched in the embroidered cushions of a chair while I watch more well-heeled tourists enter, laden with plastic bags full of the day's shopping adventure. These are not the flimsy functional bags we get with produce in the market. These are upscale bags of thick colored plastic emblazoned with the shop's name, proving that at least one section of Hanoi has traded the wisdom of Ho Chi Minh for the teachings of Madison Avenue.

Almost an hour later, Lana bursts triumphantly into the lobby, announcing that she's secured a cheap room in a place five miles from here. I let her down, reluctant to stay more than walking distance from the heart of the city. By now, both of us are on edge, tired and hungry. Compromise indicates that we should go back to the hotel where the bus dropped us off, where the prices seem less out of line now that we've investigated our options.

"Hello, again," chime the reception clerks, careful not to let their smiles become "I told you so" sneers. I'll never warm up to the beautiful clerk with long sleekly black tresses, but already I like her companion—a slightly gawky twenty-something who's anxious to practice her English, whose smile beneath her large tortoise shell glasses appears more genuine than that of the self-assured beauty standing beside her. Both the young women are easy to joke with, giggling while Lana and I deride the incompetence of their male co-workers and praise their own female efficiency. Detailing the difficulties of transport and the search for hotels seems misleading. Compared to my sojourns in other non-industrialized countries, Vietnam has been easy. I haven't yet had to ferret out the local bus or train station, haven't had to try to purchase tickets in an unfamiliar language, haven't had to elbow my way to a seat between a market bag of dragon fruit and a clutch of live pigs or chickens. In Nha Trang, the hotel staff supplied us with train tickets; almost everywhere else, some enterprising entrepeneur with a mini-van or bus has posted a sign-up sheet at tourist cafes. In some ways, our most difficult experience in negotiating travel has been the long haggle with the personnel of a bonafide travel agency in Danang. I feel a little guilty about indulging in such ease. Then I remember travel memoirs I've read, written by some visitor who did the country in privately hired cars, slept in hotels like the Metropole (where Lana and I would be lucky to be able to afford a glass of wine). Compared to that sort of traveler, we're getting a far more intimate and realistic sense of Vietnam. When I lived in China, my friends and I used to see tourists passing in their sealed air-conditioned buses while we pedaled our fat-tired bikes through the streets. "China under glass" we called that tourist version of the country. I have nothing against luxury, as long as it's not purchased on the backs of exploited labor. But sometimes it seems that in traveling, luxury can create the kind of "invisible shield" a certain toothpaste company used to claim its brand constructed between your sparkling teeth and placque. If I have to choose between an antiseptic distance from the country and a seat on a jammed bus, beside live chickens, I'll take the chickens.

Tonight it's not chickens but fish that we're in search of, specifically a certain fried fish speciality of the Cha Ca Restaurant located, appropriately enough on Cha Ca Street. This all seems a bit dauntingly generic since in Vietnamese cha ca means fried fish. But when we finally find the place and climb the stairs to the small, steamy, crowded second-story dining room, the dish itself turns out to be unique, unlike anything I've seen in Vietnam and never seen in Vietnamese restaurants in the States. It involves a sizzling skillet of bite-sized morsels of fish set right on our table with an array of tiny bowls of assorted sauces and ingredients from greens to peanuts to stir into the mix. Never mind that we're already steaming from the night's heat and don't need the addition of a skillet. Were we flaming in hell with jabs from devils' hot pokers, this meal would still taste delicious. Lana and I turn suddenly and uncharacteristically entrepreneurial, imagining ourselves opening a cha ca restaurant back home. Later, I'll find that whenever I indulge in cha ca, my stomach suffers, but I'll keep ordering it anyway, an addict sure the binge is worth the morning after, the syndrome I'll come to call cha ca stomach. Though this doesn't alter my lust for the dish, it does throw a damper on my plans to become a restaurant owner.

August 23, Hanoi

Based on my experience of an (admittedly small) collection of examples—Tunisia, Vietnam, certain sections of Shanghai, China—I'd
say that when the French colonize or otherwise control a region, they
do it well—aesthetically, at least. Hanoi, despite its noise and traffic
(which become oppressive only in the narrow side streets) is lovely:
grand old neo-classic mansions, broad tree-lined avenues, lakes dotting
the center of the city—graced by pagodas—a successful urban planning. From our hotel balcony, we look out on tiled roofs topping narrow
two-story homes weathered a pale ocher, fronted by balconies, tall doors
and a succession of equally tall windows—places that could exist in
some run-down section of Paris. The French have a way of leaving
their mark. For example, they plant trees. In Shanghai, the broad-leaved
sycamores lining the streets are known as French trees—after the hands
that brought them. The French also bring their technology and leave
behind their culture and their language. In Tunisia, where everyone
answers the phone with allo, I asked a friend what Tunisians said before the French arrived. Before the French, he replied, we didn't have
telephones.

But I don't think it's the remnants of the French that make Hanoi
so much more civilized than cities in the rest of the country. I think it's
the vision that Ho Chi Minh had in mind. Hanoi has its own life, and its
citizens are busy living it. On the path around the central lake, children
are preoccupied with flying kites, not interested in running after foreigners to shout hello. Foreigners may prime the economy, but that's
their only raison d'etre here. The city flourishes without them. Yes, at
night, there are teenagers in the darkened square beside a cafe, intently
studying the moves of Western line dances and swing, but unlike the
teenagers in Saigon, they're not affecting the latest hip Western fashions. The boys appear sweetly upright and proper in white shirts and
dress pants, the girls a little awkward behind the up-swept frames of
their glasses. There are bookstores, art galleries, people relaxing on
benches beside Hoan Kiem Lake that sits in the heart of the city, its

gracious circuit making a focal point for much of our activity and, apparently, that of the residents as well, both during the day and at night when the waters reflect the lights, and families and couples line the shores. The lake, with the tiny Tortoise Pagoda on an islet in the middle (where a street vendor sells me a little bird fashioned from recycled photographs of somebody's Kodak color print family), also makes a link with ancient history in the midst of the modern present. According to our Lonely Planet guide book, legend says that Heaven, in the fifteenth century, gave a magical sword to the emperor. He used it to drive the Chinese out of Vietnam. Later, while boating, he encountered a giant golden tortoise that seized the sword and vanished with it into the waters. The lake's name means "restored sword" since the tortoise returned the weapon to its heavenly owners. And so, we have the Tortoise Pagoda, now topped by a red star, sometimes used as the emblem of Hanoi. A bit of ancient architecture, of ancient history, a marker of just how long the region has been in conflict with China, an explanation of why Ho Chi Minh would prefer a brief subjection to "French shit" compared to Chinese. And maybe a metaphor for how the region keeps driving out foreign conquerors. Its lake may be encircled by boulevards with French trees, but under the waters, lies the sword.

Motorcades pass by, carrying diplomats. Even the police seem spiffy in their uniforms, with side-cars attached to their motorcycles. In the restaurants, there are foreigners who clearly live here, their manner conveying that aura of embassy personnel and business types. But the city has its own life and concerns. The foreigners simply fade into it. Things feel more organized here, clearer, with an atmosphere of intellectual and artistic issues. Hanoi stands as the living proof of how and why the Vietnamese won the war. I can't say how long that self-assurance will last, whether it will hold out against the economic forces of Western capitalism and joint ventures that are now assailing it. For now, at least, the economic order seems purely local. In the old quarter, each shopping street seems to specialize in its own sort of goods. The Lonely Planet informs me it's been like this since at least the fifteenth century, that the streets still bear the names of what was sold there: Silk Street, Rice Street, Broiled Fish Street, Paper Votive Objects Street, and so on. Not being able to read the language, I can't say whether the names are still accurate; I can only testify to the continuity of compartmentalization. There are blocks of shoes on racks, featuring everything from fussy 1950s gold and embroidered sandals to modern gaudily canvas thongs and more serviceable footwear. There are blocks of plastic toys, of everyday clothes mixed with traditional aodais and velvet jackets. On a street of spangled silks and dragon boots that must be opera garb, each shop displays a banner or wall hanging featuring Vietnamese characters, courtly ministers or sages, other designs—all of them red and bordered in gold like a run of brilliant flags. On the herbalists' street, we see crucified geckos. There's even a street devoted to the sale of bamboo poles and terrifyingly high bamboo ladders. On the tables of the soup street lie pieces of raw chicken with the fat oozing out. Beside them are bowls of herbs and what appear to be raisins, beans, or lotus seeds to add to the primary ingredients of chicken and broth. The French assert themselves again in the bakeries (and must have taught the pizza vendors how to make a fine crust). Given all this departmentalized commerce, it hardly seems there would be the need for an actual market, but there is one, stretching for blocks down a single thoroughfare. The market burned down a month or so ago, but already it's been replaced with adjoining tall narrow wooden stalls complete with systems of awnings, screens or wood-framed glass panels for closing each vendor's "box." Goods line the shelves, spill out onto the street where the merchants, mostly women in flowered dresses or pajama pant suits, relax on low stools. Everywhere there are signs telling what to do in case of fire.

In Hanoi, shopping is always on our agenda, partly because it's our last real stop and we're trying to acquire everything we've admired but not wanted to haul. In our own way, I suppose we're the mirror vision of those teens in Ho Chi Minh City (Saigon) sporting Western garb; we're trying to absorb and acquire bits of the culture they've thrown off. But our trip is also never far from politics so we head for the Ho Chi Minh museum, an enormous building located in a compound of parks that also houses the presidential palace (used now for receptions for foreign dignitaries), along with Ho Chi Minh's modest home (which a guard says we can't visit because it's a holiday) and the much grander building that houses Ho Chi Minh's tomb. He didn't want such a massive memorial and we've accordingly decided not to visit it. We'll focus instead on the museum—which turns out to be more than we bargained for. It's an amazing feat of graphic and architectural design, symbolic concepts organized by a Russian artist, incorporating everything from dioramic displays of Ho Chi Minh's early life to an Edsel bursting through a wall like an invasion of Western capitalism. In the museum's exhibits, the struggle of the Vietnamese for independence is linked to other struggles: the French revolution, Picasso's "Guernica," a sort of brick chimney from which red cloth rises and folds over to make a tent holding Native American artifacts, a sculpture depicting the hippies of 1960s America, another portraying slaves, and a third featuring a buddha or bodhisattva. We see the collaboration between foreign oppressors and rich locals; we learn the factors contributing to the overthrow of foreign rule—the will of the people, the planning, the fighting. Some of this is symbolic: a robe of the Chinese Mandarin hierarchy stands beside the uniform of a foreign collaborator. In the clippings from newspapers, Ho Chi Minh looks like a man who knows how to use power intelligently and to relate to the people he rules—at least that's how he appears in photos: posing with dignitaries, with delegations of the National Congress of Women in their ethnic clothes, with families and youths, or visiting the troops—sitting among them in his shorts and shirt sleeves. He really does seem to fulfill the role of Uncle Ho.

I'm a devotee of Ho Chi Minh. In the same way that Americans of my generation remember where they were when they heard the news of John F. Kennedy's assassination, I remember that I was standing in a grocery, perusing the sales signs on the shelf, when the piped-in radio news announced that Ho Chi Minh had died. Since I come from the U.S. where we so often wear our allegiances on our bodies, I shop the streets of Hanoi, combing the t-shirt piles for the ones featuring his face below the flag on front, with the words Hanoi, Vietnam on back. Presents for myself and my friends. And still, I can look beyond my heroes to examine the everyday realities they left behind. In the bathroom of the Ho Chi Minh museum, I take a photo to document the museum's attempt to teach its local clientele to conform to Western ways—in this case, flush toilets and their "proper" utilization. There's a sign above the toilet using pictures to teach the women not to stand on the seat to pee. And below that, the tell-tale mark of shoes leaving their smudged imprint on the seat, proving that the habit of squatting over holes is stronger.

In Hanoi, one park eventually leads to another. We come out of the museum to pass a square with outdoor tables and stools, a big metal tin equipped with a hose to supply beer. Down the street, there's a barber giving an open-air haircut to a small girl he's swathed in a sheet while her mother in the typical woven straw conical hat, baggy pants and a high-necked, side-buttoned blouse supervises and fans her daughter. In the pocket of green across the way, a number of old men play cards, all of them sucessful candidates in a contest for Ho Chi Minh look-a-likes.

August 24, Hanoi

At the Temple of Literature, marble turtles support stelae on their backs carrying the names of those who've earned the doctoral degree. In the face of such solid pomp and circumstance, my own doctoral piece of paper seems decidedly flimsy. The temple grounds boast a musical group who'll perform traditional melodies for the price of a donation, but in the middle of the performance we've requested, they have to stop because the wife of the president of Mali has arrived, along with her entourage, and the translators can't be heard above the music. She's a visiting dignitary, but the security surrounding her seems informally loose. Lana and I hang about the edges of her crowd, profiting from the tour provided by her translators. Nobody runs us off. Instead, the musicians wave us back to sit beside her entourage while they perform. One woman sings a kind of light opera, another presents a solo on what seems to be a set of wooden vibes suspended from a bar; finally, the group coalesce around an improvisation on an idigenous one-stringed instrument that seems a cross between a Far-Eastern guitar and a Country and Western pedal steel. The player bends the notes until Lana and I look at each other and simultaneously announce, "It's like Jimi Hendrix." While we listen, the local press snap photos. I laugh to myself, imagining my interloper face on the cover of the Hanoi gazette, as if I merited a place in the society accompanying the wife of the president of Mali. After the official crowd disperses, I insist on taking photos of the performers. They insist on including me in the snapshot. And so there I am, forever, the tourist who seems underdressed beside the traditional robes of the musicians, the white face behind the ugly glasses, trying to smile as confidently as the rest of the band.

August 24, Water Puppets

This is a truly indigenous art which began in the villages, at least as far
back as the eleventh century, and I'm sure nobody back home will
fathom my excitement, especially when I later find that all my photos
are hopelessly distant and overexposed. We're in a theatre, and there's
a stage set of a red pagoda flanked by two smaller ones, strung with a
red banner depicting dragons and other symbols in gold. An expanse of
water stretches out before it and behind that, beyond a screen, unseen
artists stand waist-deep in the pond, manipulating puppets through an
ingenious combination of long poles and strings, all of these devices
submerged and hidden under water so the audience sees only these
magically animated puppets traversing the pond's surface, a fairy tale
walk more exotic and colorful than the Christian tale of Christ's watery
rambles. The accompanying "soundtrack" of music on traditional instruments is both haunting and percussive. A series of vignettes makes
up the show. Dragons writhe and dive, spitting fireworks, fish roil the
waters, puppet children leap and tumble and splash. A fisherman chases
a fish, swims the crawl, then the backstroke after his prey. There's the
courtly mating dance of phoenixes. Then the stately procession following a son home from the university. In an agricultural moment, puppets
toss the waters in buckets, weed the rice, ride a head-swiveling water
buffalo. Fairy women, with elegant jewelry and equally elegant expres-
sions and demeanor, wave their gossamer wings. A long imperial craft
sails by with puppets plying the royal oars. At the performance's end,
the puppeteers wade out, women and men in robes of primary colors
and applaud us while we cheer them. I'm hell bent on acquiring my
own versions of this magic, but discover it's not that easy. Traditional
puppets of the normal size for stage performances command a stagger-
ingly high price in the shops. Tourist-sized puppets also require hard
bargaining to bring them within my reach. At last, I secure a pair—a
fairy woman and a fisherman bearing his basket for catching fish in
front of him. They stand now atop my old upright piano. Their strings
are still attached. I can make her fan her wings beside her peaceful

Mona Lisa smile. I can make him fish but I can't erase the constrained and worried furrows marking his face. I like to think this pained expression is not the result of wars or occupation, simply his reluctance to be forever destined to sieve the waters, to be reduced to fishing instead of smoking beside his cyclo, to have to do his job.

August 25, Hanoi

We've established a routine. Here's the street-front counter where we purchase breakfast croissants; here's where they sell cigarettes from the U.S.—or rather from America. (I began my trip answering the question "Where are you from?" by saying the United States. That often drew a blank. I've learned to say America, a more recognizable nation in English.) Next door to our hotel lies the rest of breakfast in the person of a woman with long long hair that she washes in a basin by the door. She owns a hotel-room-sized refrigerator stocked with glasses of yoghurt for which she provides tiny spoons we suspect are made, like certain other goods here, from the wreckage of U.S. bombers. We carry them off to our room and then back, a requisite recycling. Meager and informal as it is, her business operation at least features refrigeration unlike that of the bottles-of-beer woman, grey hair slicked back into a bun, who sits on her chair behind red woven plastic bags housing her goods.

In perusing the galleries, Lana has made friends with a man creating sculptures from such detritus as cigarette cartons. She's a visual artist herself and one prone to incorporating found materials into her designs, such as the temple refuse she retrieved from a heap in Ho Chi Minh City (bags of it await our return to the Business Hotel there). Visiting this man and his wife who run their gallery out of their home has become part of her routine. Today, I accompany her to admire his work, while sidestepping the two small fuzzy yapping dogs tied up inside his home. I purchase a tiny example (for only ten dollars, an impossible bargain in the Western art world). Then I'm off to the silk shops stacked hip to hip with foreigners, rabbit-warren-sized spaces solid with various styles and bargains that are not nearly so impressive as the art world deal I've just closed. Lots of hard currency gets handed over in these air-conditioned cubicles (I suspect the air conditioning is there to ensure we don't sweat up the merchandise.) "All one size in Vietnam, fits most," says one proprietor. "But not," I say, shrugging out of an enormous blouse, "if like me, you're Vietnamese-sized." I've reconfirmed my size on the ubiquitous scales along the lake, where for a pittance you can check whether noodles and cha ca dinners have increased your kilos. I tease the proprietors of the scales, challenging them to convert my metric tally into pounds.

When Lana and I reunite at the Metropole Hotel, we encounter more air conditioning and a menu whose tally would more than bankrupt our budgetary scales. The place reeks of swank. We pass up the unaffordable buffet of cold cuts, salads, French cheeses. We order one drink and speculate on whether we can splurge on a loaf of the whole wheat bread, previously unsighted in Vietnam, from the deli. The service is gracious; the other clientele exude the air of money and leisure and importance, especially money. The swimming pool area is so quiet, it's as if Hanoi's own noisiness existed in some other hemisphere. In the elegant bathroom, the maid is too busy squeezing pimples to pay attention to some ill-dressed foreigner whose pants sport the stains of travel. So I neglect to tip her, probably sealing her opinion of rif-raff gate-crashers likes myself. I've read that foreign correspondents stayed here during the U.S.-Vietnam war. The atmosphere could have been different then but now it collides nastily with my sense of the rest of the city, making the Metropole an oasis of swank out of synch with the surrounding reality. My Lonely Planet guide nicely sums it up: "The restaurant is ventilated by some three dozen ceiling fans; if they cranked them all up at once the food would get sucked into the chimney." Maybe that's why I hate the motorbikes so much; rev up enough of them and the revolution so difficultly won will be sucked up that same chimney. But I can't say every sign of so-called progress is unappealing. We stop at yet another splendorous and technologically advanced bank to garner money for our trip to Halong Bay. There's a book in which to write comments like those books at art galleries in the States. "What an impressively efficient bank," I write and sign my name and my city and the date. And feel now that I'm part of Hanoi's history, though not the sector of it I'd have expected or chosen.

Outside the bank, we're back in Vietnam. We stop to study the wares of a street vendor selling the sort of blouses the older women wear with low pockets, lacy edging and slits on the sides. We try them on and peer at ourselves in a tiny mirror where we can see one shoulder at a time. The whole neighborhood gathers, getting into the act, including the street cleaning women with bandannas tied over their noses like outlaws. Although we share no common spoken language, some things are clear: the women are assuring us that we look lovely in their country's blouses; they're delighted that we're interested in the local fashions, and more than anything, they're amused. On the way back to our hotel, we pass the usual scene of women working construction, this time hauling dirt and fixing potholes, while men stand around, loafing. The women wear conical straw hats; the men do not. I take a photo and all of them laugh. Around the corner, it's either siesta time or an unexpected collapse. The sidewalk is strewn with big woven baskets of goods still attached to shoulder-poles, the human carriers stretched out asleep on the concrete and dust beneath the trees.

August 26, On the Road to Halong Bay

When I see the guys wearing Hard Rock Cafe t-shirts enter our hotel door, I know it must mean our bus to Halong Bay has arrived, the tour we've arranged with the young men at the Darling Cafe, the only comfortable enclave of gay males I've seen in Vietnam. Our bus attacks the terrible pot-holed roads again, bridges with one lane for cars, one for trains. There's a ferry—more like a raft—so loaded its front end dips dangerously into brown waters. When the bus stops, vendors assault it, even riding the ferry back and forth to work the passengers. A woman in a conical hat with a muslin mask across her face, revealing only the tops of her eyes, stands outside the bus window, her hand extending a peeled grapefruit.

"How long, how long has that evening train been gone" is my punning take upon this ride to Halong, a bay whose mountains on tiny islands and islets are rumored to rival the craggy peaks of Chinese scrolls. And they do, with their sheer cliffs and green canopies towering first above solid settlements of buildings and then pristine to the water's edge. In the distance and fog, they resemble crowds of raindrops like the fantasy illustrations in one of my favorite childhood books, but now, in the boat meant to explore the scenery and caves, I'm hardly in the mood to appreciate them. Accessing the caves seems to mean struggling up slippery rocks of sheer cliff and stumbling down even more slippery rocks into the muck of the cave itself. And then before I can catch my breath, the guide is already off into the next chamber. I give up. I tell myself I've seen better caves, though it is interesting to be alone in this one with a warrior-faced stalactite while the thunder rumbles outside. But no cave is worth the crawl back down those steps and then the climb up the nearly vertical gangplank to the boat. At the next stop, my vertigo-ridden knees refuse to attempt the high slope of gangplank that's flapping in the rough seas, although this is the cave I most wanted to see. I forgo it, as well as a swim in the oily garbage-ridden sea. Here we are in the midst of the haunting scenery of thousands of rock isles, supposedly getting away from it all, and here are vendors in their boats, hawking Coke and crackers and cookies, shouting one dollar, one dollar. The children beg food and we try to unload our uninteresting meal on them, but they're choosy, rejecting the tomatoes and cucumbers. Other entrepreneurs row up to sell live coral they've ripped from the rocks. People live here on their little sampan-style crafts, anchoring to the rock or jamming their bamboo poles into a crevice, attaching themselves like the shellfish and coral they peel till every rock looks picked clean. Sometimes I see the tell-tale signs of their domesticity in waterside caves, on grotto "shelves" or crevices above their boats. The lights on these cliffs keep changing in the rainy dusk, first blues and greys and then, as the sun sets in the gathering storm, there are pink clouds, blue patches, a lemon-lime glow on the sea. We watch the storm assault the distance—fantastic lightning bolts slicing all the blue hues of the sky, water and rock isles. Then suddenly the wind's turned big and so have the waves. Unreassuringly, the captain looks as worried as his passengers. Incredibly, a sampan the size of a rowboat heads out to sea in the midst of this storm. The winds calm a moment, the red ball of the sun sets, and we sail into a grey wall of water where we can't see anything, neither the boat nor the rocks that were there the last time we looked. We remember the rumors of an impending typhoon. We wonder if this is it. "It's all your fault," Lana says, only half-teasingly. I do have a reputation for arriving in places at the same time as natural disasters. I've always survived unscathed, but superstitiously sometimes I think I shouldn't travel; it wreaks such havoc on everybody else. Just now I don't feel particularly charmed until we emerge from the wall of water and maneuver safely into port. The reprieve will bolster us through the inconveniences of a terrible dinner in a restaurant where there's not even a separate hole for a bathroom, just a place to pee in the corner of the kitchen, and the constant construction noise of hotels sprouting like mushrooms, our own so new it doesn't even have a name or sign which makes it particularly hard to find, though both the soap and towels have recently been used and not changed.

August 27, Halong Bay

A typhoon has indeed flirted with the country, but we're being subjected only to constant rain. No boat outings today, but the family running our hotel, who've been falling all over themselves in an effort to please, lend us a poncho and umbrella so we can walk to the barge ferry and visit neighboring Hong Gai, which seems not to have copped to tourism. Yesterday, from our boat, the town seemed much nicer, with white houses and red tiled roofs set against green hills and one section where the houses were built into the cliff, a pink door opening into rock. The town stretches a long way along the edges of the cliffs and at night its lights stud them like jewels. But today we find the waterfront mostly composed of the operations of a coal mining company, and the town itself, with narrow new buildings rising story by story, each floor only one room wide, seems as desolate as the rain. In every house, the t.v. is on and the door's open. The streets fill with the loud amplification of the same program which sounds like a karaoke contest because whoever's singing can't carry a tune. To kill time, we take shelter for a while in a semi-deserted restaurant, pretending to watch a t.v. melodrama while the family or staff and sparse clientele also watch and laugh at the sight of us watching.

Overnight Tropical Storm Harry really does hit and in the early morning a river rushes down the center of our street. Miraculously, the roads back to Hanoi are passable. In the drenched storm lights, the landscape appears lushly green, alive, running with water. The Red River, full of red soil today, is notoriously unstable, so some locales rely on ferries rather than take the chance of building bridges. Today, one section is too flooded even for a ferry, but the bus pulls in further on at our appointed spot, where workers are also building an optimistic bridge. While we wait, I share my last postcard of Seattle with our guide. It features one of the Washington State ferries—a green and white nearly block-long craft with tiers of car and passenger decks rising like a wedding cake. Compared to the oversized raft approaching slowly across the river, nudged along by what could cavalierly be called a small tug, the Washington boat resembles the Queen Mary, lacking only the imperial pomp and banners. A few yards from shore, some passengers spill off and wade, while the raft groans forward to unload its weight of trucks. Probably because our tourist mini-bus is not over-laden with bodies and a roof stacked with goods in gunny sacks and big loosely woven baskets, we get safely and efficiently across.

August 28, Typhoon in Hanoi

Solid rain. Everyone's in ponchos or makeshift raincoats fashioned from garbage bags. The cyclo drivers cover their rigs with plastic so the passengers ride inside a sort of opaque saran wrap. The sky keeps upending itself in buckets. If my metric conversions are correct, the news reports say that the city's experiencing three inches of rain every few hours, and the rain's been falling non-stop since yesterday. We can see traffic splashing past on the main thoroughfare, but on our narrow side street, the water's two feet deep and rising, spilling over the steps till it threatens the hotel lobby. We're trapped. People more foolhardy than I am wade past with their pants rolled up to their thighs, or they peddle through on bikes swamped up to the fenders. Cars and motorbikes turn back, the drivers wary of drowned engines. Next door, a small boy pulls down his undershorts and pees into the sudden river. Like everybody else on our street, Lana and I lean over the balcony to watch.

I've never owned a television, regretted that only at times when I was too tired or too sick to think, unable to summon the energy necessary to read a book. Now I'm delighted that this hotel room boasts a working t.v. with a range of channels that includes Indian melodramas broadcast from Bombay, as well as news and travel documentaries from the BBC. It's the only hotel room where we've encountered television; it's the only time we've needed it. We brew up a pot of the artichoke tea we purchased in Dalat. We settle down to spend the typhoon in front of the boob tube. The business card from the restaurant called the Five Royal Fishes swears that they deliver; maybe we'll test their promise, order out for pizza and 333 brand beer.

Ordering out is just a wishful fantasy. And by midafternoon, I'm hungry, Lana's restless. She dons her own poncho, encases her bare feet in one of the pairs of hard plastic slippers that routinely accompany Vietnamese hotel rooms. She braves the flood, while I choose the safer route of having lunch in the hotel's restaurant—which turns out to be a false front. I place my order for beef noodle soup and find the waitress has to wade into the river to procure it from a restaurant down the street. The day drags on, with the typhoon subsiding into a drizzle punctuated by repeated viewings of the same BBC science footage and interludes of Bombay stars—sexy heroines in saris and pudgy-waisted heroes, lovers whose salient glances are accompanied by swelling violins and a cast of thousands. Lana returns, nursing a host of blisters occasioned by the rub of plastic on her wet toes. I want to escape the room, but she's worried that the obviously unsanitary flood will infect the open wounds on her feet. Luckily, I'm a hopelessly optimistic romantic; I've packed a supply of condoms in case the opportunity for an intimate liaison should arise. And even though I've been happily lightening my load by discarding torn blouses and sandals with broken straps, I've refused to jettison the condoms. Now we put them to a more desperate and more practical use, pulling them over Lana's blistered toes, securing them with rubber bands. Back home in the States, we'd call this some perverted version of safe sex—the paranoid protections practiced by foot fetishists. Here, we call it simply safe walking.

Lana makes a curious sight, her toes encased inside transparent balloons like the speech of characters in cartoon graphics. But Vietnam is not the place to worry about fashion statements. With our pant legs rolled up and Lana's wounds fortified against tetanus, we set out towards a restaurant where we find that the mysteries of the service are more daunting than the typhoon flood. For the better part of an hour, we sit starving, wondering why we're ignored while the staff panders to the group of well-dressed Vietnamese across from us, a foursome who've brought their own bottle of red wine. When the waitress finally comprehends that we've ordered not only the sixty-cent fish soup, but also the specialty fish dish, cha ca, which costs a budget-breaking $3.50 a plate, there's a flurry of action and smiles, while the man in charge starts nodding appreciatively in our direction. For the rest of the meal, the waitresses mother us, returning over and over to stir the fish and greens in the pot bubbling at our table. If they've noticed the strange array of rubber-banded sacks gracing Lana's feet, they've chalked it up to eccentricity or foreign style. They're pragmatic. It's the cost of what we've ordered that matters. The real bottom line.

August 29, Hanoi

In my now somewhat jaded and cynical analysis of traffic, I conclude that the only being that truly commands the pedestrian right of way is a water buffalo. Sometimes, I see a line of them on paths with their herder, but when they wander solo across a road with no owner in sight, all vehicles halt. Today, a funeral procession doesn't halt the motorbikes, but does manage to navigate their noisy erratic flow better than I can. There's a line of praying buddhist nuns, then a man holding a large photo of the deceased. There are burgundy banners covered with glittering buddhas and designs. Two buses pass, adorned with the huge funeral wreaths composed of repeating circles of blooms in pink, blue, white and yellow, with an outer fringe of deep green leaves. The mourners, wearing white headbands, walk behind the bus that holds the casket, leaning on it as if they were pushing.

As if in some kind of synchronicity with the actual events of the present, we're on our way to a street that sells a mix of masks for festivals and multitudes of religious paraphernalia, including materials for funerals. These funeral goods are all made of paper and seem some flimsy colorful version of the jewelry buried with Egyptian pharoahs or the legions of terra cotta warriors in that Chinese emperor's tomb in Xian—things to use on the other side of life. But I think these paper artifacts are meant to be burned during the ceremony, and to provide for much more mundane needs in the after-life. There are miniature paper clothes, shoes, televisions, ghetto blasters, houses and cars. The women's set includes paper bracelets, hair clips and other feminine vanities; the men's collection holds a gun and a bow and arrow (but surprisingly no motorbike).

In addition to my traffic theory about pedestrian right of way, I have formed another one about cyclo drivers and their sense of direction, or rather lack of it. They seem not to know their cities all that well and get lost almost as often as we do. None of them can read a map, a skill I've come to understand as one intimately connected with literacy. I remember an essay I've had my writing students read about the perils of being illiterate. The essay is packed with examples but the one I've always empathized with the most relates the story of a man whose car had broken down; he'd managed to find a nearby public phone and call the police. The police were nice, he said, but when they asked him to tell them where he was, out of the maze of signs, there was only one he had learned to recognize: ONE WAY STREET. When he relayed this as his whereabouts, the police thought it was a joke.

Our problem this afternoon is compounded by the fact that the address given us for the theatre presenting an opera was apparently wrong. Eventually, we do find a theatre, although we have no idea whether it's the one we were looking for. No matter, the audience is stocked with handsomely wrinkled old women, so it must be an authentic place. It's a popular or people's version of opera. The production is low-tech so the spotlights roam the stage, searching for the actors, the mikes are bad, and all the electricity is lost at one point. Still there are "special effects": the lights blink on and off like strobes when the women dance and designs of light behind a curtain signify the dream sequences. The spangled costumes glitter and there's plenty of melodrama. The main plot concerns a young girl whose family's attacked by villains. She's sold into prostitution but valiantly holds out against evil demands. It appears that her former suitor has given up on ever finding her and married someone else. She becomes a nun and then suddenly and inexplicably the wife of a tiger king. (Whatever country you're in, opera excels in convoluted plots and my lack of Vietnamese language skills leaves me as helpless as that illiterate man on the one-way street). What's for sure is that the tiger king gets killed in battle and the heroine drowns herself. In the climax, her hand disappears last into the scarves the women dancers wave like water and then a lotus rises up.

I've never liked opera in the West, always lived in terror of soprano solos, but in China, I acquired a taste for the stylized Eastern version with its mix of pageantry, perfected gestures of little fingers and sleeves, and acrobatics. I'm thoroughly pleased with this Vietnamese performance and hungry now for dinner, which at the Piano Restaurant introduces us to further musical delights. In the Piano Restaurant (that's really its name, I'm not making this up), a violinist accompanies a woman in long earrings and a plaid logger shirt who plays the piano barefoot. Their repertoire ranges from classical to American 1940s standards. I summon up the courage to make a request for "Long Ago and Far Away," a number I remember from the well-thumbed sheet music my mother housed in the piano bench. When I name the tune, the musicians nod confidently, yes they know that one. It's a romantic song that ought to be delivered heartfeltly by some heroine in an operatic plot, but I sing along so quietly at our table that only Lana has to suffer through my off-key rendition.

August 30, Dressing for Dinner at the Five Royal Fishes

I believe in packing light. My wardrobe was meager from the start. Then I gave my pink shirt to Mai's daughter on the beach at Nha Trang, left a blue blouse with torn embroidery for the maid in Hue, abandoned my threadbare bikini along with a towel and my hopelessly stained New York, New York t-shirt in the hotel at Halong Bay. Beside my current room's wastebasket, I've folded up a pair of striped cotton pants I bought in China—still serviceable but, as the mirror in the Metropole Hotel informed me, unflattering. There's not much left to choose from, but I want to make my fashionable most of this last evening in Hanoi. I select the only skirt I've brought and a matching tank top, hoping the grease stain above the left breast won't be obvious in the restaurant's dim light. I fluff the last gasp of the so-called permanent curls in my hair and apply a swatch of burgundy lipstick.

Now, the real test. From the blue and white case where my contact lenses have resided for weeks, periodically opened only to refresh them with cleaning fluids, I select the right lens, rinse it with bottled water, then raise it hesitantly toward my eye, where for the first time in what seems an eternity, there's no trace of infection. The lens slips in, accompanied only by the sort of minor irritation I'd expect from an eye that's no longer accustomed to housing a circle of plastic. I blink, and then insert the left lens.

I don't have a good memory for either names or faces. At parties, there is always someone advancing toward me, hand out-stretched, and my memory banks fail me, supplying no name for this stranger's confident smile. Now, in the mirror, an assortment of once familiar freckles and blotches assembles itself, stretching across the planes of square-jawed bones ending in a sharp chin. My fingers, accustomed to a new habit, rise to adjust my glasses and close around nothing. Instead, I come back to the face I lost almost a month ago. Superficially, the only difference is the darker shade of tan.

I hate obvious metaphors. I don't want my eye infection and its denoument to symbolize some change in vision. That's my face in the mirror, and Vietnam remains itself, both matching and not matching the vision of the country that I arrived with. What my troubles with my eye have brought home to me is some truth about the precariousness of vision, expecially that vision we name identity. I've found that there are more versions of myself than what I thought I was prepared to live with. And there are more layers to a war—civil or foreign or both— than we usually grant. There are even more layers to surviving after peace treaties have been signed. So much of what keeps us keeping on is just the success of putting on a good front. If we have to fictionalize a bit to do that, to tell ourselves and the world a slightly "creative" story, the activity can be usefully therapeutic, as long as we're still willing to admit the truth to ourselves. I think the U.S. has told itself a number of fictions about its war with this country and still hasn't come to real terms with the truth. I think the Vietnamese probably have their own fictions, but as both victims and victors, they're more intent on what-ever they have to do to survive. Sometimes, that involves a little cre-ative fiction. Take the t-shirts that waiters wear in the Five Royal Fishes restaurant. "This character," admits one of the waiters, "doesn't really mean royal, it means sleeping. But royal sounds better."

August 31, Back to Ho Chi Minh City

The plane deposits us in the heart of Western joint ventures, and my appetite has also turned Western. I'm starving and nothing Vietnamese will satisfy me. I want something as down-home as a cheese sandwich and in the Caravelle Hotel I order one, only to be served a crustless set of white bread housing a pound of butter and something that might pass as Velveeta.

It's our day of versions of Western swank. I pass part of the afternoon in a sort of floating hotel (hauled here from Australia) with powerful air conditioning and a boutique where I investigate the swim suits, hoping to replace the worn-out one I've abandoned. That was a bikini, but this is Vietnam where swim wear is more modestly one-piece. I select a sporty blue and black striped suit, and then fall victim to the clerk's assiduous attention and flattery. "This one so beautiful for you," she says, holding up a black number with low-cut padded cleavage. I succumb and carry them both away in my designer plastic bag.

And then there's dinner at the Rex, the epitome of kitschy swank. Our plates arrive with less than thrilling fish and french fries, but the roof-top terrace is studded with caged birds, plants, statues of animals and a lit-up turning canopy like a circus.

September 1, The Sides of Saigon

Housed in the Business Hotel, we're tourists again, generic as the hotel's name and its General Tourist Soap. So we take a tourist boat ride, a short trip on the river past rusting cargo ships and the city's buildings. On the opposite shore, the scene could have been lifted from some National Geographic story about the Amazon: palms, thatched huts on stilts, wooden walkways on poles. After the boat ride, I take the local ferry out of the city's bustle of commerce and motors to the suburban wilderness across the river. People on the ferry and the outskirts of the village seem astounded, and the word goes out, "A foreigner!" I wander off the main street and get lost in a maze of muddy alleys and paths between small houses set thigh by thigh. Surprisingly in what seems an impoverished district, some are made of wood with fine shutters and doors. Some are solidly, facelessly concrete, the utilitarian material the third little pig would have used to keep the wolf out had he been born poor in the late twentieth century. The poorest feature a hodge-podge of salvaged woods and thatch and rusted metal. Everywhere, there's the sound of televisions. Everybody has to yell something or laugh at the tourist who's off the beaten path. A bevy of obnoxious little boys follow and harass me till a real English speaker is found. "What do you want, Madame?" "I want you to drive away these boys!"

On the way back, the ferry slams into the dock, apparently a harder slam than normal. People lurch. A woman selling glasses of what appears to be clear and green versions of Jello—all half-melted—spills her wares. She picks up the globs, throws them back in the glasses. I disembark beside her on what the World Bank would call the city's developing side.

For dinner, we try a different section of the aesthetics at the Rex—the first-floor restaurant approached through a passage of wicker walls, ending in sumptuous decor held up by lacquered beams. Waiters ply this luxury in Mandarin robes and caps or silk baggy shirts and trousers with sashes. On stage, a group of imperially clad musicians pluck and percussion their traditional instruments, their songs punctuated by interludes of women dancers that sometimes seem authentic in gossamer drapes and fans, sometimes remind me of a Las Vegas import, wearing tight yellow and black bodices with sexy open skirts. The dancers thrill a table of drunken Asian male tourists; one of the men dances on the stage to the obvious discomfort of the musicians. After all, the atmosphere and personnel's demeanor seem to say, it IS a classy place; one ought to observe a certain decorum. I can tell that Lana and I are underdressed and haven't ordered enough to justify our presence. Like the dancing drunk, we can get away with this probably only because we're foreign. Village-side or city-side, in Saigon I'm a misfit. If the place had shifted to match its new name, Ho Chi Minh City, at least my politics would feel at home. But I doubt such a shift will ever happen. All the winds of "progress" are blowing the other direction. The city will probably wear its new name uncomfortably forever, unless things take a ninety-degree turn and the citizens vote to have Saigon back, like the denizens of Leningrad, reinstituting St. Petersburg, the old reign of the czars.

September 2, National Day

National Day commemorates Ho Chi Minh's announcement that the French had finally left. It's also the day of his death, though for a long time this was officially set as September 3, so as not to coincide with the National Day celebrations. Flags, posters, and banners appear, but we don't see much else by way of official festivities. However, the downtown square is mobbed with balloon sellers and people and motorbikes. And along with me, there's a crowd visiting Reunification Hall, formerly Independence Hall and before that the presidential palace. The building is set in a two to three square block area, complete with park and fountains. Its roofs command a view of wide tree-lined boulevards, a refuge from the noise of the city. I pay the inflated price of entry for foreigners and hand my ticket to a man who hands me to a guide wearing the traditional ao dai. She gives me the formulaic rap concerning the small portion of the first floor I'm about to visit. (There are over 100 rooms; thankfully one doesn't have access to them all.) In its present state, the building is pure 1960s architecture: all straight lines and concrete, a cross between a college dorm or campus student union and a sprawling Midwestern ranch-style home. And in the midst of this open geometry of concrete and black and white tiles sits intricate and grandly carved Vietnamese furniture that would have harmonized more successfuly with Hue's imperial city. It's amazing to think that the president and his family really lived here in this odd mix of the traditionally aristocratic and a Big-Ten university dorm. The guide hands me off to the next one. By now, I've got the picture. All I have to do is climb a staircase and look for a female in an ao dai. "Hi, are you in charge of this floor? Then I'm your willing captive." On the second floor, there's a reception room for foreign visitors, with grandly highbacked red upholstered chairs adorned with dragon heads at the ends of the arms. A carved stand with elephant tusks symbolizes power and victory. The president's chair rests on a bit of platform so it's higher than the rest, but, says my guide, in the next room all the chairs are on equal footing. That turns out to be the reception room for Vietnamese visitors, so apparantly the locals are given at least the illusion of being on equal footing. I neglect to point out to her that the furniture in the foreign guest room is far more impressive. There are dining rooms for the president and his wife to entertain and a display of their cutlery: gold utensils with bamboo-shaped handles, silver embossed with the name of the palace. One room has forty panels of lacquer put together to make a luxurious mural. You can pay extra to have a photo taken of yourself sitting in the president's seat. First, an old man (another Ho Chi Minh look-alike) tries it; next, a small boy.

Nobody volunteers to take me to the shooting gallery and I can't find it on my own. But the third floor has two taxidermied tigers. Also its own cinema (with ancient projectors in the projection room). This area recapitulates the American rec room of the late 50s, early 60s, with curved sectional couches arranged in a semicircle, a table for card playing, a bar shaped like half an enormous beer keg and one of those recreational wall units whose orange and yellow sliding shelves can house the family's favorite board games and the stereo.

Adjacent to this floor is a heliport with a big circle marking the spot where a bomb was dropped on the day of the North Vietnamese take-over. My guide hands me off to fend for myself on the roof which has a covered wooden dance floor and a bar made of pink tiles where people sell fruit juice and soft ice cream while visitors admire the view of the city and the helicopter.

I wend my way downstairs against the flow of traffic and into the basement, which turns out to be the highlight of the tour. It really is an institutional basement, concrete and dark, stark and dank. Here's the staff combat room with the original maps on the walls indicating the sites of North Vietnamese bases. A tally of the foreign army troops includes everybody that could be thought of: Australians, New Zealanders, Philippinos, even twelve Spaniards, and, of course, over half a million from the U.S.

Next is the communications room lined with what look like ham radios, all provided by the U.S. says the guide. And in the room beyond that, telex machines which look, at best, 1950s vintage. I'm sure this stuff must be newer but in the current computer age (witness the technology of Vietnamese banks), it looks like ancient hardware. I feel like I've stepped onto the set of a World War II movie. The next rooms are empty except for a stark desk, file cabinet and chair. Then stairs lead down to security tunnels, a thickly lined corridor (the bomb shelter) which holds only a small single bed beside a table with a phone and another ham radio. The president slept here when the bombing intensified. Well, where did his wife sleep, I ask the guide. Did he leave her upstairs? The guide turns giggly and evasive: Oh, she slept in another room.

Having blundered either politically or socially or both, I'm done with this palace. As I regain the first floor, totally deserted now, a phone keeps ringing and ringing. No one answers. It seems symbolic of the place and the eras it represents; no answer from those now. I think the ruling families who occupied this palace should have known they would lose out. Anyone who'd put that imperially dragon-carved furniture on the black and white tiles of a college dorm deserves to be toppled. Even the tunnels of the opposing forces at Cu Chi must have had a more harmonious aesthetic.

2002, Henry Kissinger

It's only recently, viewing *The Trials of Henry Kissinger*, that my store of information about the war with Vietnam has taken on outrageous proportions, more facts to corroborate the cynicism I've so often felt toward the actions of my government. Based mostly on research by Christopher Hitchens of *The Nation*, the film documents the much greater cynicism of government functionaries like Kissinger—but a cynicism of a different brand than mine. Kissinger's was the sort of cynicism that advanced his ego and power at the price of countless lives. Twice he was instrumental in disrupting a chance for peace agreements with Vietnam. And in the first instance, he was playing both sides, presumably assisting the team of then-president Johnson, while delaying the peace in order for the Republicans to take power—and then, of course, ending up with a powerful position in the new administration.

Equally cynical was the massive bombing of North Vietnam just to prove to South Vietnam that the U.S. was securely behind their stated intent to support the south—what the film calls a "demonstration bombing"—a variant on the old adage, "My word is my bond." In this case, "My word is my bomb." Kissinger's now rightly hunted as a war criminal. At the end of the film, my friend shouted, "Heee's back!" like the slogan of those Halloween slasher movies—endless sequels of mayhem, guaranteed to bank the box office.

I know a good deal more now about the machinations of government than I did as a young woman marching to the satirical lyrics of Country Joe and the Fish. But even back then, my instincts were correct. They were born of the cynicism and optimism of the times: the belief that our country was on the wrong track and we could not only derail it, but give it a new, more positive direction. I've got a button now that reads "Return to the traditional values of the sixties."

September 2, Heading Home

Although we've already checked out of the Business Hotel, the propri-
etor, our Vietnamese "mama," lets us take a shower before our long
flight (and walks in on me in the midst of my wash to supply more
General Tourist Soap and a normal towel, not one of the Disney beach
towels that accompany the rooms). Lana and I sit waiting for our cab in
the hotel lobby while our mama keeps positioning the fan to blow straight
into our faces. Like any mama, she's overweaning but nice to have.
After nearly a month of bargaining for rides, at the end we've elected
to take an official metered cab to the airport, and it turns out to be
cheaper than the rest. There's only one flight leaving tonight and the
staff keep all but the bossiest foreigners waiting outside until two hours
before our flight, though we've been instructed to arrive earlier. When
the doors do finally open, nobody's working yet at the counters. I see
two women from Vietnamese customs come upstairs as the duty-free
shop opens and then emerge with their purchases in plastic bags, sneaking
back down the stairs, ducking, hiding their contraband bags behind them.

   At last, it's time to board, to prepare ourselves for the hours and
hours cramped in the air, watching the graphic of the jet on the map of
the computer-generated screen which blinkingly relates what seems a
tortoise-speed toward our eight-hour lay-over in Seoul where we'll be
vigilant and lucky enough to secure two reclining seats in a sort of
cubicle in the enormous and enormously stuffy airport where we can
pretend to sleep until the travel alarm that I've obsessive-compulsively
set sounds off. And that's only the short leg of our air-born journey. I
was wrong when I called the circumstances of arrival hell; it's the
departure that deserves the name of punishing flames.

The Moral of the Story

Actually, the title of this final chapter is pretentious. And maybe—in its promise of instructive closure—simply wishful thinking. But since my sojourn had for me something of the quality of a tale, I kept believing it needed a proper tale's ending, which, of course, involves a moral. But this is real life where tales do not end simply, and really do not end. Even in my skin, I carry a long-term reminder of Vietnam—small brown raised spots like over-eager moles, some fungus or other that my doctor calls molluscum and promises will eventually disappear. The name seems apt, recalling the clinging suck of mollusks to any rock in any weather, storm or not.

The memory of the U.S./Vietnam war hangs on like that. My friends and I have found we need to be cautious about where we wear our Ho Chi Minh t-shirts unless we're in the mood for a confrontation. We've viewed again, this time on a VCR, the Milos Forman movie version of *Hair*, that Broadway musical once considered scandalous for nudity, though I think its celebration of hippie, antiwar, anticapitalist attitudes was probably much more threatening. Watching it again, I realized the only scene I remembered came near the end, when the troops were quick-marched into the belly of a huge transport plane headed for Vietnam. Images like that don't fade, nor does the image of that first monk setting himself on fire, or the Vietnamese girl running engulfed in napalm flames, or the young woman kneeling over the body of a Kent State student shot by nervous National Guard eighteen-year-olds. Those scenes remain emblazoned on our minds, memories stubborn as mollusks. Like the much more recently celebrated photo of a student standing before the tanks in Tian'amen Square, they stand for more than themselves. And any middle-school student who's paid attention to the lesson can tell you that's the definition of a symbol. Recognizing a symbol is easy; carrying it like a fungus in your skin is easy too, though maybe annoying. But deciphering its meaning is something else.

Sibyl James is the author of three books of poetry, *The White Junk of Love, Again,* (Calyx Books, 1986); *Vallarta Street* (Laughing Dog Press, 1988); and *The Bakery of the Three Whores* (InkPot Press, 1994). In 1990, Calyx Books published her creative nonfiction work, *In China with Harpo and Karl.* Her collection of short stories, *The Adventures of Stout Mama,* was published by Papier-Mache Press in 1993. She has a Ph.D. in English and has taught in the US, China, Mexico, and as a Fulbright professor in Tunisia and Cote d'Ivoire. She served for four years on the Seattle Arts Commission and chaired the Arts in Education Program. Her work has been published in over 100 journals internationally and she has received an Artist Trust Award as well major awards from the arts commissions in Seattle, King County and Washington State.